The Scramble for Africa

PROBLEMS IN
EUROPEAN CIVILIZATION

Under the editorial direction of
John Ratté
Amherst College

The
Scramble
for Africa

Causes and Dimensions of Empire

Second Edition

Edited and with an introduction by

Raymond F. Betts
University of Kentucky

D. C. HEATH AND COMPANY
Lexington, Massachusetts Toronto London

CONTENTS

INTRODUCTION

The "scramble for Africa" is a striking example of the historian's attempt to recapitulate the historical process by means of metaphor. "Scramble" suggests rapid and confused activity and, in this particular instance, a rush forward, a sort of treasure hunt. The metaphor therefore not only tends to describe vividly, it also tends to assign values to the historical action itself. The popular conclusion has long been that the opening up of Africa in the nineteenth century was done both with great haste and with reckless abandon as European explorers, missionaries, and military men brought European politics, culture, and confusion to a hitherto largely *terra incognita*. The Dark Continent, it would appear, was suddenly suffused with light. Or, as Joseph Conrad ironically reversed the proposition in *Heart of Darkness*:

> *True by this time it was not a blank space any more. It had got filled since my boyhood with rivers and lakes and names. It had ceased to be a blank space of delightful mystery—a white patch for a boy to dream gloriously over. It had become a place of darkness.*

Historiographically, the thesis of the scramble for Africa is coincidental with the advent of the phenomenon it describes. Witnessing this final major act of European expansion, apologists—both politicians and historians—were impressed by the rapidity and near totality of the process. And so the observation of a common African experience, imposed by a rapidly investing Europe, was converted into the "classical" historical interpretation even before Africa was completely "pacified."

This observation was accentuated by the two historical approaches frequently employed by early historians of the subject. One was diplomatic and tended to center on the Berlin West African Conference (1884–1885) when spheres of influence were theoretically defined. The conference, from this first viewpoint, was seen as establishing the etiquette by which the carving-up took place, and thus became the primary event in a series of diplomatic negotiations and maneuvers by which France and England, joined by Germany and bothered by Belgium, gained the major part of their African empires. The second historical approach—the most persistent in studies of modern imperialism—was a variation of the Marxist interpretation as modified by Lenin. Here Africa was viewed as being rapidly absorbed into a capitalist system that needed new markets, sources of raw materials and places for investment.

While no historian would deny the importance of either economic or diplomatic motives in the scramble, there is now a general concurrence of opinion that these two factors varied in intensity and in significance from one region to another, and from one set of local African circumstances to another. In a few words, discrete scholarly judgment is replacing sweeping generalization. Research in the field, greater appreciation of cultural history, close scrutiny of local colonial archives and access to national archives for the period under consideration—all have taken the historian's eyes off the green felt cover of the diplomatic table and away from the corporation's account books, and have led him to scrutinize local situations, particular circumstances, and individual motives. The regionalization and chronological phases now being insisted upon are serious qualifications of the unidirectional and unrestricted expansion which earlier historians had imagined and then captured in the words scramble and *course de clocher* (steeplechase).

Another important modification has also recently taken place. If the partition remains an important European historical problem, it is now being viewed as an important African historical problem as well. Earlier interpretations treated Africa as if the land and its people were a stage or a setting in which dramatic action, both noble and mischievous, was being carried on by a number of European nationals and a variety of European interests, both private and public. The African, like Ralph Ellison's "invisible man," was ignored or ill-considered; his culture was dismissed; his historical past denied. In the words of Sir Charles Lucas, whose history of the partition is considered later in this study: "With the modern intrusion of the white man into Africa, the African natives . . . may be said to have come into light and into history."

This Eurocentric view of Africa has, of course, been found to be acutely myopic, and has been accordingly corrected so that recent interpretations tend to regard the contours of African history as well as those of European history. Consideration of African responses to the scramble has resulted in general revision, but particularly in the rejection of the earlier historical assumption that the Europeans annexed Africa as easily and as thoroughly as they printed their preferred political colors on Mercator-projection maps.

As the qualifications briefly described above indicate, the study of the partition of Africa has been considerably refined. Put another way, this history is no longer a neatly cleft or simply joined problem, but rather one of variations in intensity and scope.

Yet such recent historiographical changes have in no way deflected interest from the basic questions posed at the end of the nineteenth century: What was the catalyst or motivating force which precipitated the action? Was the action strikingly new, or rather might it have been an intensification or alteration of an already noticeable activity? Of equal importance is that variant of the age-old historical conundrum: What was the importance of individual action in the process? More particularly, what credit is to be assigned to Leopold II, or to Bismarck, or to lesser known personalities such as Charles de Freycinet or Sir Harry Johnston?

The older list was recently lengthened with questions raised about the attitude of the "official mind" (the mind-set prevalent within the British ruling establishment), the distinction between "informal" (trade) and "formal" (territorial) empires, and the effects of resistance movements such as that led by Menilek II of Ethiopia against the Italians or that of Samory against the French in Senegal and the Sudan.

It is therefore not surprising that historical interpretation is now complex. The magnitude of the subject—for it embraces two continents and several cultures—warns against smug generalizations and reductionist interpretations. Yet any initial appreciation of the problem requires a few introductory remarks of a descriptive sort.

While Europe had maintained knowledge of and trade with Africa throughout its history, these were of a peripheral sort. Obviously North Africa had for centuries been an integral part of the Mediterranean world, but the hinterland of Africa south of the Sahara remained a mystery to Europeans until the modern era. Ignorance and arrogance were combined to create tales of romance and of grotesque exaggeration which were but slowly dispelled in the nineteenth century when explorers, sponsored by philanthropists and merchants, penetrated the continent from several points.

Nonetheless, between 1876, when Leopold II founded the International Association for the Exploration and Civilization of Central Africa, and 1912, when the French declared a protectorate over Morocco, all the principal European nations but Austria established their political dominion over the entire African continent, with the notable exceptions of Liberia and Ethiopia. This rapid absorption, so strikingly in contrast with previous European political interests, induced the use of the word scramble. The center of academic discussion, because it is the area in which the competition was most intense and dramatic, has been the Congo basin. This was the area in which Leopold II made his bid for empire, and it was the area in which converging political and economic activity aroused sufficient concern to initiate the Berlin West African Conference, presided over by Bismarck and attended by all major European powers and the United States. When Henry Stanley spoke of the "Dark Continent," he made reference to this region.

No doubt it was Stanley, himself an able publicist, who awakened much of Europe to the possibilities of this part of the world. In a famous letter to the London *Daily Telegraph,* dated 1877, he did his best to advertise the Congo:

> *I feel convinced that the question of this mighty water-way will become a political one in time. As yet, however, no European Power seems to have put forth the right of control. Portugal claims it because she discovered its mouth; but the great Powers—England, America and France —refuse to recognize her right. If it were not that I fear to damp any interest you may have in Africa, or in this magnificent stream, by the length of my letters, I could show you very strong reasons why it would be a politic deed to settle this momentous question immediately. I could prove to you the Power possessing the Congo, despite the cataracts, would absorb in itself the trade of the whole enormous basin behind. The*

river is and will be the grand highway of commerce to West Central Africa.

In the following year, the French republican statesman Léon Gambetta commented to Stanley: "What you have done has influenced Governments—proverbially so difficult to be moved—and the impulse you have imparted to them will, I am convinced, go on growing year after year."

Since this time, no critic of the partition has totally ignored Stanley's role nor, for that matter, has anyone tended to exaggerate it. One of the obvious problems has been to provide it with a proper context, to account for it intelligently—and not romantically—as only one, and not necessarily an essential one, of the several European actions which led to the scramble.

But these actions were expressed in other locales as well. Anglo-French rivalry in the region of the Niger River and again in the upper reaches of the Nile indicates the geographical extent of European competition and the complexity of the academic search for a unifying cause or coherent historical pattern.

As generally observed historically from the European position, sub-Saharan Africa was the diplomatic *champs de manoeuvre* of the European powers, the region in which perhaps quick acquisition and serious, but not vital, political activity could be indulged in. Most European-directed writers work within a triangular framework: the relationship of Anglo-French activity and rivalry in Africa, to the diplomatic activities of Germany, to Leopold's attempts at empire. National interests, in which economic factors figure, are considered the important provocative ones, with the general result that the partition of Africa is summed up as an overseas manifestation of European rivalry.

Yet the historical appreciation of this rivalry has been extensive. Value judgments range from the laudatory, in which European action is seen as a civilizing force, to the harshly realistic, in which Africa is described as the "bottom of the barrel," the last major available area for European territorial acquisition on the cheap. More importantly, the notion of the "new imperialism" in which Africa figures as the primary example has been carefully reviewed in recent years. Historical continuity, or at least a historical prologue in the form of

MAP 1
Africa in 1879

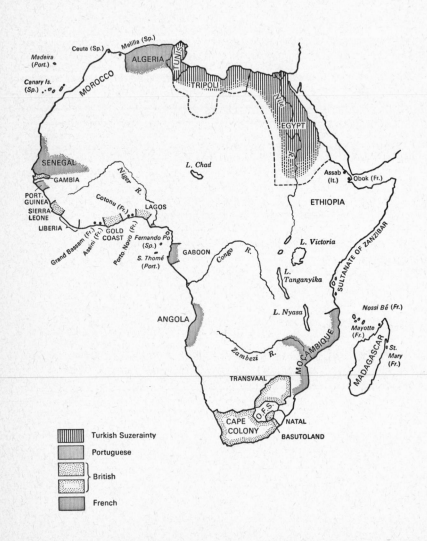

Madeira (Port.)

Canary Is. (Sp.)

Ceuta (Sp.) Melilla (Sp.)

ALGERIA

TUNIS

MOROCCO

TRIPOLI

EGYPT

Nile R.

SENEGAL

GAMBIA

L. Chad

PORT. GUINEA

SIERRA LEONE

LIBERIA

Niger R.

Cotonu (Fr.)

LAGOS

Grand Bassam (Fr.)

Asini (Fr.)

GOLD COAST

Porto Novo (Fr.)

Fernando Po (Sp.)

S. Thomé (Port.)

GABOON

Congo R.

Assab (It.)

Obok (Fr.)

ETHIOPIA

L. Victoria

L. Tanganyika

SULTANATE OF ZANZIBAR

L. Nyasa

ANGOLA

Zambezi R.

MOÇAMBIQUE

Nossi Bé (Fr.)

Mayotte (Fr.)

MADAGASCAR

St. Mary (Fr.)

TRANSVAAL

CAPE COLONY

O.F.S.

NATAL

BASUTOLAND

▦	Turkish Suzerainty
▨	Portuguese
⬚	British
⬚	French

MAP 2
Africa in 1891

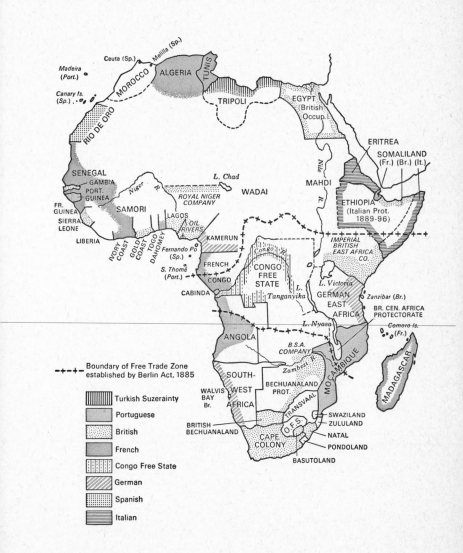

Madeira
(Port.)

Ceuta (Sp.)

Melilla (Sp.)

Canary Is.
(Sp.)

MOROCCO

ALGERIA

TUNIS

TRIPOLI

EGYPT
(British
Occup.)

RIO DE ORO

SENEGAL

GAMBIA

PORT.
GUINEA

FR.
GUINEA

SIERRA
LEONE

LIBERIA

SAMORI

L. Chad

Niger R.

ROYAL NIGER
COMPANY

WADAI

MAHDI

ERITREA

SOMALILAND
(Fr.) (Br.) (It.)

ETHIOPIA
(Italian Prot.
1889-96)

Nile R.

LAGOS

OIL
RIVERS

IVORY COAST

GOLD COAST

TOGO

DAHOMEY

KAMERUN

Fernando Po
(Sp.)

S. Thomé
(Port.)

FRENCH
CONGO

Congo R.

CONGO
FREE
STATE

L.
Tanganyika

IMPERIAL
BRITISH
EAST AFRICA
CO.

L. Victoria

GERMAN
EAST
AFRICA

Zanzibar (Br.)

CABINDA

BR. CEN. AFRICA
PROTECTORATE

Comoro Is.
(Fr.)

L. Nyasa

ANGOLA

B.S.A.
COMPANY

Zambezi R.

MOÇAMBIQUE

MADAGASCAR

SOUTH-
WEST
AFRICA

WALVIS
BAY
Br.

BECHUANALAND
PROT.

BRITISH
BECHUANALAND

TRANSVAAL

CAPE
COLONY

O.F.S.

SWAZILAND

ZULULAND

NATAL

PONDOLAND

BASUTOLAND

–·–+–·– Boundary of Free Trade Zone
established by Berlin Act, 1885

Turkish Suzerainty

Portuguese

British

French

Congo Free State

German

Spanish

Italian

MAP 3
Africa in 1914

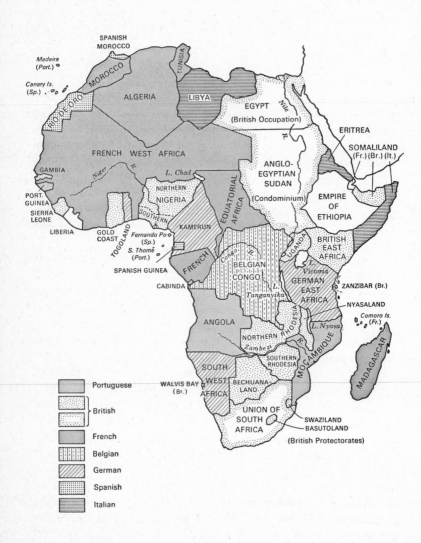

SPANISH
MOROCCO

Madeira
(Port.)

Canary Is.
(Sp.)

RIO DE ORO

MOROCCO

TUNISIA

ALGERIA

LIBYA

EGYPT
(British Occupation)

Nile R.

ERITREA

SOMALILAND
(Fr.) (Br.) (It.)

FRENCH WEST AFRICA

ANGLO-
EGYPTIAN
SUDAN
(Condominium)

GAMBIA

Niger R.

L. Chad

NORTHERN
NIGERIA

EMPIRE
OF
ETHIOPIA

PORT.
GUINEA

SIERRA
LEONE

SOUTHERN

EQUATORIAL
AFRICA

LIBERIA

GOLD
COAST

TOGOLAND

KAMERUN

Fernando Po
(Sp.)

S. Thomé
(Port.)

SPANISH GUINEA

FRENCH

UGANDA

BRITISH
EAST
AFRICA

Congo R.

BELGIAN
CONGO

L. Victoria

CABINDA

*L.
Tanganyika*

GERMAN
EAST
AFRICA

ZANZIBAR (Br.)

NYASALAND

Comoro Is.
(Fr.)

ANGOLA

RHODESIA

NORTHERN
RHODESIA

Zambezi R.

L. Nyasa

MOÇAMBIQUE

MADAGASCAR

SOUTHERN
RHODESIA

WALVIS BAY
(Br.)

SOUTH
WEST
AFRICA

BECHUANA-
LAND

UNION OF
SOUTH
AFRICA

SWAZILAND
BASUTOLAND

(British Protectorates)

	Portuguese
	British
	French
	Belgian
	German
	Spanish
	Italian

preconditions, such as European trade patterns in West Africa, has been suggested; and accident, or at least unintended involvement, has been suggested in conjunction with diplomatic calculation.

While the first study in this anthology bears none of the hallmarks of modern historical objectivity, it does reveal a perspective contemporary to the partition of Africa itself. Emile Banning's *Partage politique de l'Afrique,* published in 1888, is an unmitigated eulogy of European activity in Africa. Banning himself was involved in the partition as an active supporter of Leopold II's colonial policy and as a late nineteenth-century European who did not doubt the cultural superiority of Europe. Within his interpretation of the partition there is no place for the notion of a scramble. He viewed European expansion as an orderly, civilized, and generally peaceful nineteenth-century process, of which the Berlin West African Conference of 1884–1885 was exemplary. Quite obviously, Banning's personal and national involvement gives his work greatest value as a "mirror of the times," at least as a reflection of those popular sentiments which allowed many Europeans to assess the acquisition of African empire as something within the glorious circle of noble deeds.

J. Scott Keltie, writing a half-dozen years later and from England, has presented in *The Partition of Africa* the first notable historical analysis of the phenomenon and to this day one of the most useful appraisals. Although its British bias is at times apparent, Keltie's work can be said to include all those general factors which remain dominant in subsequent studies. In opposition to Banning, Keltie does see a scramble taking place and even employs the word. However, he also insists upon the importance of earlier activity in Africa (one of his chapters is entitled "Sixty Years of Preparation") and thus tries to place the partition in a broader historical context, both geographical and chronological. As he remarks in conclusion: "It is over 3,000 years since Phoenicia began to nibble at the Continent; this nibbling process went on until 1884. In the last eight years there has been a mad rush, and nearly the whole of the Continent has been gobbled up." Keltie sees the particular reasons for this sudden ingestion as three: (1) the exploratory work of Livingstone and Stanley; (2) King Leopold's activity in the Congo; (3) Germany's sudden intrusion in African affairs, which really caused the rapid scramble. Yet Keltie certainly does not discount other less immediate but significant factors; he particularly stresses the economic one in which glutted markets and national commercial rivalry assume dominant positions. Thus, before the expiration of the nineteenth century and, more important, before the end of the period of partition, Keltie had offered an intelligent if broad interpretation, and one which has subsequently worn quite well.

The work of Sir Charles Lucas follows in this tradition and actually offers little that can be called unusually new in interpretation. Here, too, the importance of preliminary work has been recognized. For Lucas, exploration and antislavery movements were the influential activities just prior to the partition. But Lucas emphasizes more strongly than Keltie that the scramble owes much of its origin to the outcome of the Franco-Prussian War. With the experience of World War I behind him, and hence perhaps with a painful awareness of the ill-effects of national rivalries, Lucas argues that, after 1870, Germany in victory and France in defeat turned toward Africa, the former now an expansionist state seeking outlets for her energy, and the latter looking to Africa as an area in which to recoup her losses. Conflicts of interest with England subsequently occurred.

The obvious perspective which Lucas and all post-World War I writers enjoyed led to a heightened interest in the influences of European national rivalry and power politics on imperialist policy. Among the many authors who have written on this subject, two are of considerable importance in any historical appreciation of the partition of Africa. Both A. J. P. Taylor and Sybil E. Crowe, English historians, have manifested a particular interest in the role played by Bismarck's Germany.

Taylor's is the most striking interpretation of those so far considered. While he provides a sweeping summary of the purposes and conditions of modern European imperialism, his chief concern is with Bismarck's colonial policy, not with the partition itself. Hence *Germany's First Bid for Colonies, 1884–1885* is of direct importance because it is an attempt to explain the motives of one of the few pivotal figures in the history of the partition, Bismarck. According to Taylor, it was Bismarck's attempt to approach France diplomatically which projected Germany into Africa. Here he quarrelled with England over "ownerless lands" with the hope of effecting a Franco-German entente. Taylor's conclusion is that the German acquisition of colonies in Africa was initially the accidental outcome of Bismarck's European diplomacy.

Miss Crowe's *The Berlin West African Conference* provides a sound background analysis of prevailing European activities in Africa and then suggests that the Anglo-German rivalry and the Berlin Conference itself were the results of an African misunderstanding—over Angra Pequena on the west coast. Without this occurrence there is no reason to assume Britain and Germany would have fallen out. In her assessment, therefore, Bismarck's purposes become less sure and calculated than they appear in Taylor's. Of greater interest than this variation, however, is Miss Crowe's evaluation of the Berlin West African Conference. She dispels all the myths which have hung historically over that event by proving that it neither induced the partition nor assured its regulation.

In the last decade interest in European colonial activities in Africa has increased, and a number of books have sought meaningful reappraisals. None has been more influential or striking than the volume authored by Ronald Robinson and John Gallagher, *Africa and the Victorians.* These British scholars deny the newness of the scramble and purposely avoid portraying it as the singular result of entirely different late nineteenth-century conditions. Briefly recapitulated, their argument is this: traditional British political concerns with empire, stemming from the days of Pitt and Palmerston, brought Britain into Egypt; increased European tension over the Egyptian question, following upon the British occupation, "dragged Africa" into the zone of European rivalry; hence the scramble began.

The attractiveness of the argument cannot be denied, and the care with which it has been considered is commendable. In contrast to the underlying premise of most interpretations of the partition—its suddenness due to new European conditions—Robinson and Gallagher see the result as more an accidental by-product of traditional British policy. Needless to say, the argument has not gone unchallenged, and this book contains the most intelligent and reasoned refutation of it, that offered by the Belgian historian Jean Stengers.

As with Robinson and Gallagher's book, Stengers' review is difficult to label neatly. It includes incisive appreciations of African history, but also rests heavily upon an interpretation of European diplomatic history. However, as a reply to *Africa and the Victorians,* it is presented next in this anthology. Stengers asserts the need to concentrate on European activities on the west coast of Africa. For him, the immediate causes of the scramble are compounded of de Brazza's French-sponsored activity in the Congo and of the French intensified movement in the Niger region which caused a frightened British reaction. Yet he is also concerned with the development of a new climate of opinion in Europe, an atmosphere which made African imperialism something of a popular issue.

The most persuasive new interpretation to appear in the last few years, and one that also refutes in part the thesis of Robinson and Gallagher, is found in the article written by C. W. Newbury and A. S. Kanya-Forstner, "French Policy and the Origins of the Scramble for West Africa." Indicating that radical change in policy occurred a few years before the initiative usually described as beginning in 1882-1883, the authors carefully analyze the shift from informal empire based on trade to formal empire based on military acquisition. Such change was first suggested after 1840 as a result of the French conquest of Algeria and through the person of Louis Faidherbe, who served as governor of Senegal and who urged military expansion into the region of the Sudan. When Faidherbe's scheme was revived in the form of governmentally inspired policy in 1879, the resultant action became the cause of the scramble in this area.

The recent critical controversy over the origins of the scramble, which was initiated with the appearance of the Robinson and Gallagher volume, is expressive of the keen contemporary interest in European expansion and in African history. Now the African setting and reaction to the scramble have become factors of great importance. While this "decolonization" of history has not drastically altered the continental European factors contributing to the partition, it has discredited the generalization of uniform and unrestricted European intrusion upon which assumption the word scramble commonly rested.

Although most of the fruitful study of African history is of very recent vintage, an awareness of the need for an appreciation of African history can be traced back a goodly number of years, and most distinctly, to a short study written in 1923 by an outstanding French scholar of colonial affairs, Georges Hardy. In *Vue générale de l'histoire d'Afrique,* Hardy insists that the African past "ought to merit

more than disdain." He further insists that Africa should be seen as a
historical unit and, therefore, he questions the propriety of the division along the lines of the Sahara. Within his study the partition is
viewed as an important phase in the development of African history:
that foreign intrusion which led to a certain stabilization of African
societies, then in a state of dissolution. While, for Hardy, the partition
takes on the aspects of a scramble (he employs the word "rush"), he
closely relates this sub-Saharan activity to European penetration of
North Africa. Europe, in his opinion, used North Africa as a base of
operations. Yet what gave the partition its immediate impetus was
most particularly the growing industrial rivalry in Europe. If at this
point his argument follows well-grooved channels, Hardy nonetheless
offers a wider historical dimension in his insistence on the importance of African resistance as a conditioning factor in the partition.

Whatever its shortcomings, *Vue générale de l'histoire d'Afrique*
had the double advantage of shifting attention to the local setting and
of attempting to assess the importance of that setting. As a result,
the history of the partition of Africa acquired better proportions which
have appeared subsequently in other studies.

It has been chiefly in the last decade, coincidental with the emergence of African nations, that histories of Africa have become relatively plentiful. The contemporaneity of these works suggests that
a chronological ordering of them would not be very purposeful;
hence those cited in this study have been arranged according to
their topical treatment. The first two are general histories, like
Hardy's, in which the scramble is but one aspect. The next three are
restricted in scope, and revisionist in theme; they reveal the intensity
of modern African historical scholarship and the need for further
such historical reconsideration on a regional basis.

As an introduction, no single volume yet excels *A Short History of
Africa,* written by two British Africanists, Roland Oliver and J. D.
Fage. However, the approach to the partition found in this book is
not strikingly different from that offered by Keltie, for instance.
Leopold and Bismarck's Germany are singled out as the chief cata-
lysts, and the significance of European diplomatic entanglements,
particularly in Egypt, are briefly considered. The particular thematic
modifications the authors offer are found in their deemphasis of
economic factors and, more significantly, in their insistence that the

first phase of the partition was made in Europe and essentially on paper, while the actual occupation and control of African territory occurred later, and not very peacefully.

If this study combines the established interpretation of the scramble with an analysis of local African influences and conflicts, Endre Sik's polemical *Histoire de l'Afrique noire* goes further. While it rigidly adheres to a Leninist interpretation of modern imperialism, it suggestively breaks through to a new dimension by reconsidering the pattern of African national liberation movements. For Sik, indigenous opposition was as important a factor as European penetration: it first slowed down Europe's control of Africa, and it secondly gave the African people a certain sense of solidarity and an awareness that European power could be resisted. More importantly, he considers such opposition as the first phase in the movement of national liberation and thus a constant political factor in modern African history.

Both of the studies just mentioned suggest in broad terms the contemporary interest seriously expressed by historians in African responses to European imperialism. A concern with local political interaction, ranging from negotiation to conflict, has intensified in the last several years and emphasizes the meaningfulness of John Hargreaves' admonition that historians must view nineteenth century African states as something other than "curious museum pieces."

One of the early examples of this new scholarly appreciation was provided by Kenneth Onwuka Dike, among the first and foremost Africanists of African origin. His illuminating study, *Trade and Politics in the Niger Delta,* is concerned with the historical development of this region in the fifty years preceding the scramble. Offering an intelligent evaluation of the effects on the coastal states of the English shift in trade from slaves to palm oil, Dike demonstrates the importance of a local African balance of power undergoing change.

Further elaboration on the varieties of African political attitudes toward the Europeans and indications of the manner in which African states partially determined the boundaries of European colonies are found in two recent complementary studies. The article by Saadia Touval, "Treaties, Borders and the Partition of Africa," argues that treaty negotiations often bore the marks of contractual obligations which in part reflected African interests and political problems. The idea of totally arbitrary European assignments of political definition to Africa is thus questioned, and the significance of the West African Berlin Conference is thus indirectly reappraised. In "West African States and the European Conquest," John Hargreaves enumerates the many types of political relationships assumed by the Europeans toward African states and asserts that the most effective African positions were assumed where strong political entities existed and offered what might be called "national resistance."

This particular theme, which will no doubt continue to be more fully stressed in contemporary African history, is already given broad consideration in the concluding article by A. B. Davidson. In a Marxist-oriented historical review which treats the struggle against colonial domination as a constant, not a recent reaction, the author also offers a charge to historians to "decolonize" African history. That the article was originally a paper delivered by a Russian Africanist to an International Congress of Africanists meeting in Tanzania in 1965 befittingly suggests the new international appreciation of the scramble.

The metaphor of scramble has by now revealed its inadequacies, and yet the historical treatment of the problem it describes will still demand further consideration. No isolated occurrence, the partition was actually the most important political development in the modern era of African history, a development which, in turn, had further significance in suggesting the future lines of African political and social patterns. Of equal importance, the partition was the climax of the expansionist phase of European history, a phase which began as long ago as the fifteenth century and the first adventurous maritime explorations. As an historical problem, whatever its affixed label, the partition of Africa has a deep yet immediate significance, one which no alert citizen of the twentieth century can afford to ignore.

Note: Authors' footnotes in the following selections have been omitted for reasons of space.

I THE PROBLEM FROM THE EUROPEAN HISTORICAL PERSPECTIVE

Emile Banning

THE PEACEFUL PENETRATION
OF AFRICA

Emile Banning was archivist of the Belgian government at the time he wrote his study of the partition. An active supporter and collaborator of King Leopold II, Banning desired Belgium to become a colonial power and urged the King on in the Congo. Banning's study, from which the following excerpt is taken, is chiefly a justification of the Berlin West African Conference which he attended as a member of the Belgian delegation.

Few epochs will hold a place in history comparable to that of the century which is ending. Despite some symptoms of lassitude which the contemporary generation revealed, despite the weaknesses and deceptions of which no period in the life of humanity is exempt, outstanding results and essential changes have been accumulated in all branches of activity and human thought, to the point that the mind is staggered by their weight and importance. The visible entry of Africa into the empire of civilization, the distribution of its vast territories among the nations of Europe, the initiation, under European guidance, of millions of Negroes into superior conditions of existence truly seems to be one of the most considerable revolutions of our time, one of the richest in economic and political consequences.

This activity began with the century and through three highly significant undertakings. At the head of the first figured that indefatigable mover of men and ideas who bore the name of Bonaparte. The expedition to Egypt was both a geographical and historical revelation. Since 1798 Egypt has become a European province, inseparably associated with the fortunes of the great western states. At the same time that it was disclosing the secret of its monuments and its tombs, and while their testimony was renewing our knowledge of high antiquity, the valley of the Nile became the stage of completely modern activities. The point of departure or arrival of the first important discoveries directed toward Abyssinia, the West and Meridional

From Emile Banning, *La partage politique de l'Afrique d'après les transactions internationales les plus récentes, 1885 à 1888* (Brussels, 1888), pp. 1–7, 154–159. Translated by Irene and Raymond Betts.

Sudan, Egypt was equally to become, by means of the Suez Canal, the great route of maritime navigation to the Far East.

The definitive occupation of the Cape by England in 1815 produced analogous effects, but on a smaller scale, at the extreme south of the vast African continent. The site of the Cape, which up to that time had served only as a port of call and supply, became the embryo of a colony toward the development of which were applied the resources of a great commercial power. A new base of operations was organized, and little by little its activity was felt up to the banks of the Orange and Zambesi rivers.

Beginning in 1830, the conquest of Algeria by French arms created a third center of attack, a new and powerful source of infiltration of civilizing influences. The task was bloody and laborious. Here it was not with the Negro and fetish-worshipping populations that the French clashed, but with the Arab and Moslem populations. Yet success was not long in doubt, and Africa, breached on three points of the triangle that it forms, became henceforth the object of a regularized, uninterrupted and almost always peaceful conquest.

It was toward the end of this first period of thirty years that the great voyages of exploration were organized. Begun at the end of the last century by Bruce and Mungo Park, they were continued without interruption from René Caillié and Clapperton up to Nachtigal and Stanley; and they included—only to mention the names of the most illustrious—explorations by H. Barth and Schweinfurth, Livingstone, Burton, Speke, Grant, Rohlfs and Cameron.

Up until the middle of this century, almost all of the African interior remained yet to be explored, but despite extreme difficulties and continued dangers, the exploration advanced with an extraordinary rapidity. To measure the effect of this forty-year accomplishment, contemporaries have only to recall the map of Africa that they studied in their youth.

Nevertheless, world public opinion hardly noticed this work of giants. Outside of the circle of geographic societies—and there was only a limited number of these—African questions awakened no response. The press ignored them; governments accorded them only a passing interest. But the remarkable initiative taken in 1876 by the King of the Belgians changed the entire outlook. The conference which was convened under his presidency in the month of September

Columbia Presenting Stanley to European Sovereigns.

ITALY. BELGIUM. ENGLAND. FRANCE. GERMANY.

FIGURE 1. An idealized pictorial interpretation of Stanley's role in the partition of Africa. Source: Frontispiece from James P. Boyd, *Stanley in Africa* (New York: Union Publishing House, 1889).

of that year, and the meeting at the palace of Brussels of seven of the most celebrated travellers who had just recently returned from the theater of their discoveries, struck the imagination. Both what had been done in Africa and what remained to be done was now grasped. For several years, *L'Association internationale africaine* held public attention by the expeditions in which Belgian explorers brilliantly undertook their first campaigns.

The return of Stanley in 1877, after his remarkable crossing of Equatorial Africa, gave the signal for the foundation in the following year of the Congo enterprise. From the west coast as from the east coast, deep penetrations were directed toward the interior. The last obstacles gave way before this persistent effort. A dozen years ago the central core—of a size larger by one-third than Europe—was still an immense emptiness on our maps. Today it is the very heart of the Congo Free State, from which agents trek in all directions into the vast empire by means of one of the most admirable water systems which exist on earth.

This fact, which is the expression of colossal progress in geographical science, at the same time characterizes a revolution achieved in ideas. The persevering energy of the King of the Belgians had made the African question the first order of business in Europe and kept it there. The impetus given to the imagination was general. Governments could no longer abstain; rather, it was to be more feared that certain of them would hasten precipitously to make up for lost time. Each one felt, and some among them clearly saw, that a new continent and new races were going to collaborate in the civilization of the world and basically modify the balance of universal interests.

The convocation of a conference at Berlin in 1884 by the imperial government of Germany was the result and the sanction of this movement. The six great powers of Europe, the seven other maritime states, and the United States, all took part in it. This great assembly marks precisely the point where the scientific work found its complement in political action, where national enterprise came to cooperate with individual initiative.

The Berlin Conference fulfilled a double task: it endorsed the creation, in the very heart of Equatorial Africa, of a great interior state, commercially open to all nations, but politically shielded from their competition. It also set up the bases for economic legislation which was immediately applicable to the central zone of the continent but which virtually demanded more extensive application. These regulations, inspired by the most liberal ideas and discarding all whims of selfish exploitation, will protect both the natives and the Europeans in their relations with the colonizing powers. The conference also upheld the principles—justly dear to our age—of religious and civil liberty, of loyal and peaceful competition, and it broke with the antiquated traditions of the former colonial system.

Three years have lapsed since the promulgation of the act of the Berlin Conference and already the political and economic thought which formed the bases of its clauses has been many times applied in Africa. Germany, England, France and Portugal have rivalled each other in activity in this area, while remaining faithful to the spirit of understanding and justice and to the reciprocal concessions which had dictated their common resolutions. The partition of Africa on both sides of the equator . . . was achieved peacefully, with neither trouble nor jolts, and without any of the onerous and bloody conflicts which accompanied and noticeably impeded the colonization of the two Americas. . . .

. . . The African enterprise rests on broad foundations. One can see with what vigor in action, scope in plans, and concern over their consequences all of Europe is involved. Never has the assault on a new continent been pursued by such a group nor has it been better organized in its details. Nothing of the sort happened in America or even in Australia. Where would the new world be today, what leaps forward would it have taken, if, at the end of the sixteenth century, an American conference could have done for it what the Berlin Conference has done for Africa? But the thought could never have risen. For it to have been possible and practical, the modern development of international law as well as the great progress of science and technology were necessary. The European nations had to become capable of collective action and able to place at the service of the common idea the enormous industrial and financial power of our age. From this ensued the grandiose evolution which we have witnessed and of which the glorious fruit will be the redemption of a continent and a race.

. . . The political situation which was produced in Africa by the cooperative action of the governments realized a thought which was already apparent since 1876 and which even then appeared to be the future solution of the problem. Each of the principal maritime peoples established itself in the area which best suited both its interests and its means of action. While engaging in this national activity, each of them fulfilled a social mission, spread abroad the germs of culture, created the sites for the spread of ideas, of which the rays converged on the common center. A similar plan, an identical tendency dominated them to a higher goal.

Thus the league of civilization was gradually organized in the conquest of virgin nature and heathen races. What was truly new in this conception, what has an original quality, was the role assigned to Belgium in this peaceful crusade. Belgium owes this role both to the generosity of its King and to the sympathy of the powers. If the Congo State is nowhere mentioned in the act of the Berlin Conference, it is understood in every article. It was in effect an essential idea in the general idea of which the regeneration of Africa was the object. The

attack from the center is necessarily correlative to that which occurred from the diverse points of the circumference. The European
states coordinated their activities with the action of the central
power. Its foundation and development reveal the closest rapport
with the others.

From this point of view the Congo State, in some respects, took on
the aspect of an international institution: it served as the connecting
link and the pivotal point for the establishments on both coasts. The
efforts of the other powers were the guarantee of its success, in the
same way that it cooperated in the activities of the others, endorsed
their expansion, consolidated the results. All progress accomplished
in the central state had its repercussions in all the colonial establishments which surround it, just as every conquest achieved in the maritime regions soon affected the interior. It is impossible to separate
the two orders of activity without simultaneously compromising both.
Whoever loses sight of the whole, whoever attempts to favor particular development to the detriment of general development hurts himself and condemns himself to emptiness. The theater is too narrow
for anyone to isolate himself with impunity. Never on any point of the
globe has the joint action of peoples appeared to the same degree as
the principle and guarantee of their success. Who harms one does
injury to all; who facilitates the total plan comes to the aid of each
one. The Congo State will prosper or fall reciprocally with all the
colonial creations which envelop it.

This was a unanimous conviction at the Berlin Conference. Experience has confirmed it with each step and will contribute more
and more to center on this point the sentiment of those men who are
attracted to the study of this great problem. Here is strikingly revealed the immense superiority of the modern formula of colonization
over those of previous centuries. Mercantile selfishness has been
replaced by the impetus of a much higher order. National interests
are reconciled with universal interests in a synthesis of which the
final result will be to give to the world another continent; to production, the resources of a wealth and variety scarcely glimpsed; to
militant humanity, a new family whose native faculties have already
caused considerable surprises and which will reserve, after a century of culture, a goodly number more for future generations.

Sir John Scott Keltie

THE SCRAMBLE AFTER YEARS OF PRELIMINARY ACTIVITY

Sir John Keltie was both geographer and journalist, as well as secretary of the Royal Geographical Society. His study of the partition has the attributes of serious scholarship. The subject was still new and without synthetic interpretation in English when Keltie produced this work in 1893. As might be expected, given the extent of English involvement in African affairs at the time of the writing, the study is inclined in the British direction and carries a number of admonitions to the English government for its lack of foresight in African affairs.

Three quarters of a century ago, when Europe was at liberty to start on that career of progress in all directions, which had had undreamed-of results, her African possessions consisted of only a few factories and stations and towns on the coasts; effective occupation hardly existed beyond the seaboard; the heart of Africa was an unknown blank; the serious occupation of the continent as a whole, as America and Australia were being occupied, was probably unthought of. Germany, in the modern sense, did not exist; Holland was satisfied with her great colonies of culture; France had hardly bethought herself of fresh colonial expansion; England had quite enough occupation for the energies of her surplus population, and for her commercial adventurers, in Canada, Australia, India, and the East. Africa she valued mainly as affording stations to guard her route to her great Asiatic empire. . . .

. . . The progress of partition among the European powers had been comparatively slow and insignificant during the sixty years that had elapsed since 1815. Germany as a colonizing power had not yet set foot upon the continent. Great Britain had certainly pushed her influence and jurisdiction northwards from the Cape as it stood in 1815, but it was reluctantly and slowly. Her west coast colonies were mere patches. True, her influence was felt extensively in the Niger region and in the Zanzibar dominions, but it was unofficial and

From Sir John Scott Keltie, *The Partition of Africa* (London, 1893), pp. 93–94, 111, 114–118, 122–123, 134–136, 138, 159–163, 164, 204–206.

unsecured by treaties. Her supremacy in Egypt had been more and more marked. France was the only power that showed any eagerness for steady annexation and any foresight as to future contingencies. In short, the great struggle had not yet begun; but it was imminent. Stanley's memorable journey across the continent, and especially his discovery of the great Congo waterway, may be regarded as the initiatory episode. . . .

. . . It might be said that when Stanley started on his memorable journey across the Dark Continent in 1875, the whole civilized world had an interest in the results of his expedition. Letter after letter from the great explorer, and telegram after telegram from the heart of Africa, as to the fate of the expedition, served to fan this interest and kindle it into a world-wide enthusiasm.

To the work accomplished by Stanley more than to that of any other explorer it is due that this somewhat abstract enthusiasm for Africa was, in the space of a comparatively few years, precipitated into action on the part of the states of Europe. But that action did not come for some time, even after Stanley had emerged from the Congo. He had hardly got well into the continent ere there was action of a kind, but that action did not result in annexation; this came soon enough, and when it did come, it came with a rush. There is little need here to recount the story of an expedition in many respects among the most remarkable which ever entered Africa. Stanley himself is a man of action, and will carry out his purpose at all hazards; he is no mere abstract geographer or general philanthropist. As with all great men of action, his deeds beget deeds on the part of others. No man knows better than he how to nerve his fellowmen to action. His letters from Uganda, describing with dramatic realism his long interviews with the clever if somewhat artful Mtesa, roused Christendom to enthusiasm. At once an army of missionaries, English and French, was sent out to take possession, in the name of their Master, of one of the most powerful kingdoms in Central Africa. This may indeed be said to have been the first tangible result of Stanley's journey—a result which was not without its influence in the final scramble.

Stanley was still in the heart of Africa when a movement was initiated, which may be regarded as the beginning of the ultimate partition of the continent among the powers of Europe. All eyes, as we have seen, were turned to Africa, even before Stanley had started

FIGURE 2. An artist's rendition of the famous encounter of Stanley and Livingstone in East Africa, 1871. Source: Frontispiece from Josiah Tyler, ed., *Livingstone Lost and Found, or Africa and Its Explorers* (Hartford: Mutual Publishing Company, 1873).

to complete the work of Livingstone. The colonial aspirations of Germany were being awakened. She was still flushed with the fruits of her great victory over France. She was now a united empire, bent on achieving what Germans would call world-greatness. New energy had been infused into her commercial life. Her merchants were on the lookout for fresh fields; their eyes were eagerly turned to the East and to Africa. But at present the only action was that taken by private adventurers; Bismarck had more important matters demanding his energies. It remained for another potentate to inaugurate a movement which, within fifteen years, was to make Africa little more than a political appendage to Europe. When Stanley's first letter came home, Leopold, King of the Belgians, was in his prime. He was just forty years old, and had been on the throne of Belgium for ten years. The King was then as he is now, a man of restless energy, ambitious of distinction for himself and his little kingdom, greatly interested in the promotion of commerce and the arts, and with a special love for geography. The field for his energies as the sovereign of a small, neutral, and comparatively poor kingdom was limited. He had no great army, no great fleet, no ever-recurring political complications to engage his attention outside his own domain. It was natural that a man of his energies and ambitions should wish for a sphere of more cosmopolitan action than he could find within his own borders, or even in Europe. Possibly also he desired that as his kingdom could not, by any chance, be great politically, it might at least expand commercially; if it could not stretch its limits in Europe, there was a whole continent, almost unoccupied and untouched, in which he and his people might find abundant room for their surplus energies. There is no need to attempt to fathom all the motives of the King of the Belgians in summoning to Brussels on the 12th September 1876 a select conference to discuss the question of the exploration and the civilization of Africa, and the means of opening up the interior of the continent to the commerce, industry, and scientific enterprise of the civilized world. But in summoning the conference the King indicated his desire that it should consider what measures might be adopted to extinguish the terrible scourge of slavery, which, though put a stop to on the west coast, was known still to continue its desolating influence over wide and populous tracts in the interior of the continent.

It is difficult to forget all that has happened during the sixteen years that have passed since this memorable, this epoch-making, meeting in Brussels. Have we any warrant in concluding that the King of the Belgians had at first in view the ultimate creation of a great African empire, of which he himself would be the head, and which might place Belgium on a level with Holland as a colonizing power? It is hard to say; probably His Majesty had not formulated to himself any very precise scheme. It must be remembered that in September 1876 Stanley was on his march from Lake Tanganyika to Nyangwé, and that as yet he had not looked upon the wide Lualaba, which he was destined to trace down to the Atlantic as the Congo. The King of the Belgians, when he convened the meeting of geographers and philanthropists, knew no more about the Lualaba and its ultimate destination than did any one else who took an interest in Africa; and, indeed, his attention was not directed to West Africa at all, but to the east coast and to East Central Africa. The King had probably no more idea of what would be the ultimate outcome of the meeting than had any one else who took part in it. The object he professedly had in view he had a right to conceive as a noble one. In the initiation and direction of an organization for opening up the long-neglected continent to science, industry, and civilization, there seemed ample scope for his energies and philanthropic aspirations, and for that craving for distinction which kings share with ordinary mortals. If we may judge by subsequent events, underlying these philanthropic aspirations were motives of a somewhat grosser nature, but natural enough in the breasts of kings. It must be admitted that had His Majesty's design been carried out as he planned it, we should have learned more about the heart of Africa in a few years than had been done during the four centuries that have elapsed since the Portuguese began to creep down and around its coasts. But human nature and national jealousies were, as might have been expected, too strong for combined and disinterested international action and for the philanthropical aims put forward by the King. . . .

The truth is that, so far as the exploration of Africa goes, much more was done by the National Committees than by the International Commission. This is also true of the opening up of the continent to commerce and civilization, so that the National Committees, rather than the International Commission, must be credited with having brought about that scramble among the European powers which, in a very brief period, resulted in the partition of Africa. To the work of the English African Committee, independently of the association, reference has already been made. Their work was purely a work of exploration. The French and Italian National Committees seem to have contributed little or nothing to the central funds; they too were of [the] opinion that they could best carry out the work which the King of the Belgians had in view by sending out expeditions of their own to those parts of Africa in which they were most interested—Italy in the Abyssinian and Shoan regions, and France in the regions to which her Gaboon colony gave access. Even the Swiss Committee reserved a portion of their funds for specific Swiss undertakings, while the only other committee that seems to have done any real work was that of Germany. . . .

While Mr. Stanley was pushing his way up the Congo, and beginning the work which issued in the founding of the Congo Free State, events were taking place which threatened at one time to checkmate him, and render abortive the aims of the King of the Belgians. Count Pierre Savorgnan de Brazza, Italian by birth and parentage, was born in 1852. He received his education in France, and entered the French naval service in 1870. In the years 1875–1878 he, in company with M. Marche and Dr. Ballay, carried out a successful exploration of the Ogové River to the south of the Gaboon, in the hope that it would turn out to be a great waterway into the interior. This hope was disappointed, for after a certain distance the stream became broken by cataracts, and rapidly declined in volume. De Brazza crossed over the hills at the head of the Ogové, and soon found that this formed the water-parting between that river and another which flowed in an easterly direction. This he found to be the Alima, and when he reached it, Stanley had but just arrived in Europe from his momentous voyage down the Congo. Had de Brazza followed the Alima he would also have found himself on the great river, far above its cataracts, and would almost surely have been tempted to see where the magnificent waterway led to. But at the time he had not heard of Stanley's great discovery, and as his health was shattered and his means exhausted, he returned to Europe with the reputation of a determined and successful explorer.

Like Stanley, de Brazza did not rest long in Europe. Fortunately Stanley had almost a year's start on his French rival; the former left Europe in January 1879, the latter in December of the same year. De Brazza by this time knew that the Alima and the Licona, which he also touched on his previous journey, must enter the Congo. As the agent then of the French Committee of the International African Association, and with funds provided by them, he went out to the Ogové to plant civilizing stations. Indeed, it was announced at a meeting of the Paris Geographical Society before de Brazza started that his object was to explore the region between the Gaboon and Lake Chad. So it was given out, though there can be little doubt that de Brazza's aim from the first was to reach the Congo. That he lost no time in carrying it out is evident from the fact that on 7th November 1880 he, on his way down the river, came upon Stanley pushing in the opposite direction. Stanley at the time knew little about de Brazza. The latter had founded an "international" station on the Ogové, and rapidly crossing over to the Lefini (the Luvu of Stanley), found no difficulty in following that river down to the broad bosom of the Congo. He seems to have been able to establish friendly relations with the chiefs and people around, and succeeded in discovering one chief who, according to de Brazza's own report, claimed to be suzerain of all the country around, even to the south bank of the Congo. Thereupon, on 1st October 1880, the representative of the International Association made a solemn treaty with the chief, whereby the latter placed himself under the protection of France, and accepted the French flag. De Brazza lost no time in crossing over to the south side of Stanley Pool, and there founded a station at Ntamo or Kintamo, close by where Leopoldville now stands, and which his admirers in France named after him Brazzaville. The station on the Ogové he himself named Franceville.

It will thus be seen that M. de Brazza had cast aside all pretense of carrying out the designs of the International Association; he was simply the emissary of France, doing his utmost to steal a march on Mr. Stanley, and secure the mastery of this magnificent trade route into Africa for his adopted country. . . .

So far as France was concerned, it was evident that by this time the international features of the enterprise, initiated by the King of the Belgians, were entirely abandoned; and so it was indeed in the case of all the nationalities which took any active part in the work. Indeed, the international character of the association can hardly be said to have existed beyond the first Brussels meeting; it rapidly degenerated into a national scramble. The doings of Mr. Stanley and M. de Brazza on the Congo were clearly bringing African affairs to a crisis, and intensifying the political character of the expeditions which were now entering the continent on all sides. . . .

Let us briefly resume the position in 1884. Up to that year the great European powers in Africa were England, France, and Portugal. This last power claimed enormous territories, but her influence was feeble, and her actual occupation of the most limited character. The idea of joining her east and west coast possessions by a broad band across the continent had only been hinted at. England had virtually agreed to consent to her taking possession of the strip of country from 5°12′ to 8° south, including the mouth of the Congo. The Congo Free State did not exist, and the King of the Belgians could only be regarded as the chief of a semi-private enterprise of a pseudo-international character. France was firmly established in Algeria and Tunis. She was rapidly extending her conquests from the west coast toward the upper Niger, and had carried her Gaboon territories over an immense area down to the Congo. She had latent claims to one or two points on the Gold Coast, and was struggling to bring Madagascar under her sway. At Obock, on the Red Sea, she had a *locus standi,* but not much more. Great Britain was practically supreme in South Africa up to the Orange River and Delagoa Bay. She believed no power would dream of questioning her claims to Damaraland and Namaqualand as her sphere of influence—a phrase, however, which can hardly be said to have existed then. At the same time it must be said that there were serious thoughts at the Cape of abandoning Walfish Bay entirely; and that was the only position actually occupied by the Cape authorities. The Damaras were in a chronic state of war, and the few whites in their territories in constant dread of attack.

Preparations were already on foot to include the whole of Bechuanaland, for the commission to Sir Hercules Robinson to look after British interests in that region was issued in February 1884, possibly instigated by the correspondence which had already passed between the Foreign Offices of London and Berlin.

On the west coast England held on half-hesitatingly to her four colonies, while the Niger Company was extending its influence on the river and buying out all rivalry. In Nyasaland missionaries and traders were fairly at work extending and consolidating British influence. Many settlements had been planted on the borders of Matabeleland, and British travellers were opening up a country about which we could learn little or nothing from Portuguese sources. At Zanzibar British influence was supreme, though German traders were doing their best to supplant English goods by cheap continental wares. The Transvaal was still in a state of irritation against the British government; her borders were unsettled, and even so far back as 1874 and 1878 she had toyed with the idea of a German protectorate, which, however, was now beyond her reach. Egypt was fast losing hold of the Sudan; Italy was casting covetous eyes on Tripoli, while her travellers were exploring Abyssinia and Shoa. Spain can hardly be said to have established her footing on the Western Sudan coast though she claimed rights on the river Muni.

Such was the position of affairs in Africa when Germany entered the field and precipitated the comparatively leisurely partition of the continent into a hasty scramble. Prince Bismarck was still the *de facto* ruler of an empire which had grown in unity and strength and wealth since its birth at Versailles in 1871, whose merchants were finding new markets all over the world, whose people were emigrating in thousands every year to strengthen the colonies of Britain; she was fretting under the conviction that without foreign possessions it could never be considered a great world power. Germany was tired of a stay-at-home policy.

Cataclysms do not occur in the history of humanity any more than they do in the physical world. Those who care, and are competent to look beneath the surface, have no difficulty in discovering that what seems an unaccountably sudden event or catastrophe is simply the natural and inevitable result of forces that have been accumulating and growing in intensity over a long period of time. The world at large was astonished at the apparently inexplicable outburst of colonizing zeal on the part of Germany in the early period of 1884; and none were apparently more surprised than the British Foreign Office and the government of the Cape, though both might well have been prepared for what occurred. As has already been pointed out, the desire to possess colonies is no impulse of recent birth in Germany. Two hundred years ago Prussia had established herself on the Gold Coast, and would have remained there had all her energies not been required at home; and even Austria, it has been seen, made her one solitary effort to acquire a footing in Africa at the end of the last century. In Germany, as in other European countries, after the Continent had had time to recover from the Napoleonic incubus, as population increased competition became more and more intense, as discontent with their condition spread among the lower strata of society, the fever for colonization laid hold of the country. There was really no Germany then, no united and powerful empire with surplus wealth and surplus energy to acquire colonies for itself. Moreover, even fifty years ago, when the migrating spirit began to increase in strength, all the new fields of settlement most suited to Europeans were occupied by other powers. The United States, Canada, Australia, the Cape, were crying out for colonists; there was room for millions of fresh incomers, with an almost perfect climate, a soil that had only to be scratched to yield the richest harvests, and rumors of boundless stores of gold. It is no wonder, then, that the discontented surplus population of Germany flocked for the most part to the United States, and a small proportion both to Australia and the Cape. But even fifty years ago there was a feeling in Germany that Germans ought to have some place beyond the seas of their own to which they might go; that it was a pity for her sturdy sons and lusty daughters to be utilized simply to infuse fresh vigor and enterprise into colonies in which the Anglo-Saxon race is dominant. We find, then, those Germans interested in colonization trying experiments on various parts of the earth, including lands already occupied by their English cousins. It is not surprising that Africa does not seem to have been thought of, for Africa, fifty years ago, was, it must be remembered, all but unknown beyond its seaboard. . . .

The events of 1866 gave an impulse to the colonial movement in Germany; but far more so the results of the war with France and the reconstitution of the German empire, under the hegemony of Prussia, in 1871. Into the various causes which contributed to give this intensely forward impulse to Germany it is unnecessary to enter; all the scattered energies of Germany in the direction of colonization, as in other directions, were united into one strong current. . . .

By the time the Berlin Congress met she was fairly in possession at the Cameroons, as well as in Togoland and South-West Africa. She had thus begun the "scramble for Africa," had entered upon that game, some rules for which it was partly the design of the Congress to lay down.

Following the example of Germany, the other great European powers made a rush upon Africa. Inextricable difficulties were sure to arise unless some rules were laid down on which the great game of scramble was to be conducted. Germany had already made important acquisitions on the west coast, and England and France had made haste to snatch up the remainder. France and Portugal were struggling with the King of the Belgians on the Congo, while Portugal was beginning to be alarmed as to her claims on other parts of the continent. Great Britain had received a severe lesson at Angra Pequena, and had at last been aroused to take measures for securing to herself the region which lies on the north of Cape Colony. Already there were agitations as to German interests in Zanzibar. The great struggle, however, it was seen, would be round the center of the continent, and it would be for the advantage of all concerned that an understanding should be come to as to whether it was to be divided up into exclusive sections, or whether it was to be open to all nationalities, whatever might be their share of the rest of the continent after the scramble was over.

It has been seen already that Bismarck strenuously objected to the Anglo-Portuguese arrangement as to the coast at the mouth of the Congo; he would never consent to the key to such an important highway being placed in the hands of Portugal. The arrangement was, indeed, received with such determined opposition by the powers, that it had to be dropped, and curiously enough the proposal for an International Conference to consider the whole question of the Congo came from Portugal herself. France endorsed the proposal, which was cordially taken up by Bismarck on behalf of Germany. This was in June 1884, and a month later Lord Granville gave in his adhesion on behalf of Great Britain. These three powers agreed in principle to the creation of a Free State in the basin of the Congo, the precise limitations of which were, however, to be left to separate agreements between the powers directly interested. The great purpose then of the Berlin Conference was to come to an understanding with reference to the Congo basin. It was also agreed to make some arrangement with reference to the Niger, and to fix the conditions under which new annexations would be recognized as valid by other powers. . . .

Sir Charles P. Lucas

THE SCRAMBLE AND FRANCO-GERMAN NATIONAL PROBLEMS

Sir Charles P. Lucas, the first head of the dominions department of the Colonial Office (1907–1911), was both a civil servant and a historian. His short volume on the partition originally appeared as a series of lectures.

Reprinted from Sir Charles P. Lucas, *The Partition and Colonisation of Africa* (Oxford, 1922), pp. 77–83, 86–89, 96–97, 100–105, by permission of the Clarendon Press, Oxford.

Much like Keltie's interpretation, it does however offer a post-World War I perspective and carries the partition down to its conclusion.

At the time when Stanley verified the course of the Congo, and the interior of Africa in its main features became finally known to the world, only four European nations (not counting the Turks as a European nation, and excluding the Boer states) had possessions on the continent, Spaniards, Portuguese, French, and English. The Spaniards had very little footing. The Portuguese had long fallen from their high estate, but still owned much territory and claimed more, on the west, Angola, and, much farther north, the small tract of Portuguese Guinea, on the east from a little below Delagoa Bay to Cape Delgado. The two active and progressive powers in Africa were the two old rivals, France and Great Britain. Both had various holdings on the west coast, neither had any on the east coast from north of Natal to the mouth of the Red Sea and hardly any there. On the north coast France was firmly planted in Algiers; Great Britain, on the contrary, had no place. In the south France had no footing, while Great Britain was unchallenged except by the Boer republics inland.

In giving the date of Livingstone's life and death, it was pointed out that he was born two years before Waterloo and died two years after the Franco-German War. There was a reason for mentioning these wars. Each of them for the moment crushed France, and after both the French, with their wonderful power of recovery, set themselves to gain new ground, to compensate for what they had lost, and, since they were already established in Africa, very naturally they looked there for new gains to set off the old losses. Thus the immediate prelude to the scramble for Africa was not only the discoveries which gave something to scramble for, but also the Franco-German War, and this for two reasons. The war unified Germany, and history would seem to teach that, when a country has achieved its own salvation and stands erect and free, it discovers a mission to spread that salvation to less favored lands; unity at home is followed by expansion abroad. For example, the union of Aragon and Castile and the conquest of the Moors was speedily followed by the Spanish-American Empire. Our own empire arose after the island of Great Britain had at length been united under one Crown. The United Netherlands gave birth to a great Dutch Empire overseas. United

Germany obeyed the law, not through the designs of statesmen, for Bismarck was not in love with oversea ventures, but under pressure of public opinion. United Italy, one of the great results of the Franco-German War, followed suit and joined in the rush into Africa.

The second reason has been mentioned already. France wished to recoup herself for the loss of Alsace-Lorraine, and Africa, where she was already well placed, was an obvious and open field. Further, there was this important factor in the situation. While Germany took good care of herself in the parcelling out of Africa, German state-craft, in the earlier stages of the scramble, was by no means hostile to French claims and aspirations in Africa. They tended to distract French attention from their lost provinces at home, and to result, as they did result, in renewed rivalry between France and Great Britain, and in a diversion of French bitterness from Germany to Great Britain. Moreover, they made bad blood between France and Italy, and this again suited German designs.

Before the scramble began, France and Italy were the first two powers to gain ground in Africa during the memorable decade of the eighties. The year 1880 is usually given as the date when Italy se-cured her first African foothold, at Assab Bay, north of the French Obock on the Red Sea coast. In 1881 the French greatly extended their position in North Africa by declaring a protectorate over Tunis, adjoining Algeria—a protectorate which the Italians, who had strong interests in Tunis, bitterly resented and for a long time refused to recognize. But other intruders were about to take the field.

In September 1876, while Stanley was on his journey across Africa, Leopold, King of the Belgians, called a meeting at Brussels of geog-raphers, explorers, and philanthropists, who agreed to form an Inter-national African Association for exploring and civilizing Africa and putting down the slave trade. The King himself became President of the association. It was in no sense a meeting of Government repre-sentatives, but well-known men from most of the leading European nations, including Great Britain, took part in it. It was decided that a national committee in each country should collect money for the common cause. As a matter of fact, these national committees for the most part went to work on their own account, and such money as was collected was principally Belgian money and mainly subscribed by King Leopold. The association met again in 1877 and adopted a flag, and one or two unsuccessful expeditions were sent out. But before 1877 ended Stanley came home, having achieved his object and cleared up the Congo mystery; the King at once tried to get into touch with him, and did so at Brussels in June 1878. In November 1878 it was decided to establish a special committee, styled the Comité des Études du Haut Congo, which was apparently at first regarded as a branch of the International Association; plans were made, a small fund was raised, and Stanley went back to Africa as the committee's representative. So far the international character of the proceedings was maintained, and the money subscribed was not entirely Belgian money. But, even before Stanley reached the Congo, the foreign subscriptions were being returned and the enterprise was passing exclusively into the hands of the King of the Belgians, though there was still an international flavor in the scheme and indeed the committee later took the title of the International Association of the Congo. Stanley arrived at the mouth of the Congo in August 1879 and went up the river exploring, making treaties with native chiefs and founding posts. He returned to Europe in August 1882, was persuaded to go back to the Congo in the following December, and came back again to Europe in June 1884, his position, which was now tantamount to that of a Governor, being taken by an Englishman of high character and standing, Sir Francis de Winton.

The Congo Committee had not been left alone in the field. A French explorer, de Brazza, had, in the years 1875–1878, crossed from the Ogové into the Congo basin, but had not reached the Congo itself. He went back to France, went out again at the end of 1879, commissioned by the French Government and the French Committee of the International Association, struck the Congo in 1880 and, like Stanley, whom he met but kept in the dark as to his proceedings, made treaties, obtained concessions, and founded posts. He arrived back in France in the summer of 1882, later in the year the French parliament endorsed what he had done and voted money to confirm his work, and this it was that sent Stanley back to the Congo at the end of 1882. Eventually the French maintained themselves on the northern bank of the Middle Congo, and the Congo Association and what came out of it held the southern bank.

In old days the only European power that had interests in the coast region of the Congo was Portugal. The Portuguese had discovered the mouth of the river, and for a time a native kingdom of the Congo was a great scene of Portuguese "penetration" and of missionary enterprise. Later, the Portuguese left the Congo and concentrated farther south in Angola, but as late as 1783 they built a fort at Kabinda, north of the mouth of the Congo (from which they were within a year ousted by the French), and they consistently maintained a claim to the coast as far north as 5°12′ south latitude, thus including the mouth of the Congo and Kabinda. This claim was as consistently opposed by Great Britain, who would not admit Portuguese rights north of Ambriz in 8° south latitude. Great Britain was especially concerned in the matter because she was especially interested in putting down the slave trade. The activities of Stanley and de Brazza alarmed the Portuguese, and again they pressed for a recognition of their claim. After negotiations, which began in November 1882, Great Britain and Portugal signed a treaty in February 1884, by which Great Britain recognized the Portuguese claim on the coast, giving her the mouth of the Congo and a certain distance inland short of where Stanley had been operating, but insisting that the navigation of the Congo should be free to all nations. To this end the Congo was placed under an Anglo-Portuguese Commission, the Portuguese having refused an International Commission, which the British Government originally suggested. This treaty roused universal opposition. British merchants and philanthropists strongly objected to extending the Portuguese sphere, the French Government at once refused to accept the treaty, the Congo Association obviously did not want Portugal to have the mouth of the river; the Germans supported the French. The Portuguese, seeing that the treaty was doomed, turned to France and Germany with a suggestion for an International Conference; the treaty was formally given up; Germany, in concert with France, in October 1884, invited an International Conference to meet at Berlin. It met in November, and eventually the famous General Act of the Conference was signed on the 26th February 1885.

This Berlin Act, which was signed by all the powers interested in Africa and others also, fourteen powers in all, was a most important step, and full of promise for the future. It provided for freedom of trade in the widest sense in the Congo basin and for free navigation of the rivers. It also provided for a wider free trade zone, extending to the Indian Ocean, but conditioned by the consent of any independent state within the zone. It provided for the neutrality of the Congo basin which was placed under international protection and surveillance, for the well-being of the natives, and for prevention of slave-trading. It provided, too, for free navigation of the Niger, and it enacted that powers making future annexations in Africa must give due notice to other powers, and that their occupation must be effective. . . .

We have seen that the great Conference of 1884–1885 was invited by Germany in concert with France, and that it was held at Berlin. In other words, the power which took the lead in the meeting so vitally concerned with the destinies of Africa was a power which, prior to the eighties, owned no African possession whatever. Individual German explorers, missionaries, traders, had long been active in Africa, but until 1884, the actual year of the Berlin Conference, the German Government had no definite footing on the continent. Then the German Government and the German nation not only made an entry into Africa, but from the first played a leading role. In order to understand how this came about, we must bear in mind what was happening at the time in Great Britain.

In 1880 Mr. Gladstone swept Lord Beaconsfield out of office and came into power, as an opponent of the imperialism of the late Government. The beginning of his term was marked not only by no further aggrandizement, but by an actual retreat. There was withdrawal on the Afghan frontier, and, in Africa, retrocession of the Transvaal in 1881, after the Boer War and Majuba. Then came the Nationalist rising in Egypt, and in 1882, after a proposal to France for joint intervention, which France refused, there came British intervention in and military occupation of Egypt. We no doubt intended to come out of Egypt again as soon as possible, the Government gave their word to that effect, and there is no reason to doubt their good faith. But Egypt could not be left to anarchy, and the British occupation became indefinite, involving the most bitter feeling in France against Great Britain. Thus it came to pass that, whereas, among the European powers which had territorial interests in Africa when Germany came on the scene, Spain, Portugal, France, and Great Britain (Italy, as we have seen, having hardly begun her African career), the only one which could have offered effective opposition to Germany was Great Britain; at the precise time when Germany was assuming a conspicuous place in the African sun, the Government of Great Britain, notwithstanding its avowed principles and pledges against aggrandizement and annexation, became deeply involved in Egypt, as it already was in South Africa. The position was embarrassing and even damaging, for it attracted toward Germany the only other strong power in Africa, France. This is the key to what followed.

German missionaries had for many years been at work among the natives of South-West Africa, north of the Orange River. German traders followed, and there came a demand for the protection of these German subjects. In 1877 Sir Bartle Frere had advocated annexing the whole of the coast from the Orange River up to the Portuguese boundary, but nothing was done beyond annexing the harbor of Walfish Bay in 1878. Bismarck, urged by his countrymen, put it to Great Britain whether she did or did not claim the coast, and whether she would or would not take responsibility for the security of the Europeans in this region. There was a long interchange of notes, neither Great Britain nor the Cape Colony was willing to shoulder the responsibility and expense, and no definite answer was given, with the result that, in August 1884, a German protectorate was formally proclaimed over South-West Africa. In the previous month, July 1884, the German flag was hoisted in Togoland and in the Cameroons, and, before 1884 ended, Germany had got her foot into East Africa, though as yet no German protectorate had been formally proclaimed on this side. Great Britain, throughout, was reluctant to take any forward move, anxious to eschew any appearance of jealousy of a newcomer, and content to assert the existence of British interests at this or that point, without taking really effective steps to safeguard those interests, either by annexation of, or protectorate over, the region in which they had grown up. Thus, before the Berlin Conference, Germany was firmly planted in Africa, and by summoning the Conference, she showed that she did not mean to play second fiddle there. So the scramble came to pass. . . .

. . . By the end of 1891, in the course of ten years, the partition of Africa among European powers had in the main been established. The Republic of Liberia was independent, so was Morocco, so virtually was Abyssinia, in spite of the Italian claim to protectorate over it. Tripoli was still a Turkish province; the Sudan had revolted from Egypt; some of the Sahara coast, and some central regions, had not yet been fully appropriated. In the following period . . . some vital changes will be noticed, and many minor modifications by numberless boundary agreements; but the map of Africa, as it stood in 1914, had in most respects been drawn by 1891. The powers which before 1880 held African possessions, Spain, Portugal, France, and Great Britain, had all increased their possessions, France and Great Britain very largely. Two new powers, Germany and Italy, had pegged out very wide claims, the Congo State had brought in Belgians, and eventually Belgium as a nation. This International State was the center point, the core, of the whole partition. Its origin followed immediately upon the practical completion of African discovery, and it came into being in the basin of the last of the great African rivers to be traced from source to mouth. The power which had perhaps the greatest say in the partition was the newest comer, Germany, fresh from her successful unification in Europe. In spite of the territorial additions which accrued to the British Empire, the partition was not to the mind of Great Britain, and was in no small degree at the expense of Great Britain, especially on the eastern side of Africa.

*　　*　　*

In the story of the partition of Africa, the period 1891 to 1914 falls into two distinct sections, the dividing line being at the end of 1904. The years 1891 to 1904 were years of war in Africa. Over and above minor expeditions and much local fighting, these years saw the reconquest of the Sudan, the war between Italy and Abyssinia, the South African War, and the prolonged war between the Germans and the Herreros in South-West Africa.

First let us deal with Egypt and the Sudan. In 1898 the battle of Omdurman and Lord Kitchener's entry into Khartoum completed in the main the recovery of the Sudan, which was placed under joint British and Egyptian control. No place was given to Turkey in the condominium, on grounds explained by Lord Cromer in *Modern Egypt,* that the possession or repossession of the Sudan was achieved by conquest, in which Turkey had no hand, whereas Great Britain as the predominant partner was directly involved. The Fashoda incident is still fresh in the memory. The British arrival at Khartoum coincided with the appearance at Fashoda, higher up the White Nile, of a small French colonial force which, under the command of Major Marchand, had come across from the French Congo. Thus French and British were directly opposed on the main Nile. After much friction the outcome was an Anglo-French agreement, signed in March 1899, by which the French were finally and definitively excluded from the Nile basin, the boundary line being drawn between Wadai on the west and Darfur on the east, Darfur being left in the British sphere of influence and Wadai in the French. This agreement barred a farther west to east expansion by the French. Germany had already been explicitly barred from extending from the Cameroons into the Nile basin by an Anglo-German agreement of 1893 and, except that German East Africa included half the Victoria Nyanza, which is the ultimate source of the Nile, and for the leases mentioned in the last chapter, which gave the Congo State access to the Nile basin, the whole of that region passed exclusively under British control. The leases in question, first granted in 1894 and subsequently modified in 1906, had been coupled at first with a corresponding lease from the Congo State to Great Britain of a strip of territory between lakes Tanganyika and Albert Edward, secured with a view to giving Great Britain continuous communication between South and North Africa, and providing a route for the Cape to Cairo railway. This lease, however, was strongly opposed by Germany and had to be dropped. Thus the different powers barred one another's progress. Portugal, as we have seen, tried to make good a claim to a transcontinental belt, which would have cut across British northward expansion, but which in the event Great Britain cut through. Great Britain barred French eastward extension to the Nile, and Germany barred British continuity from south to north. We shall come later to one more illustration of this sort of thing. Meanwhile, to return to Egypt and the Sudan, the exact boundaries on the eastern side with Italian Eritrea were settled by a series of agreements.

It has been said that the Italians had asserted a kind of protectorate over Abyssinia. Italy claimed that, by a treaty of 1889, the Abyssinians had placed their foreign relations in her hands, a claim which was tantamount to a protectorate. Some years later Italy and Abyssinia came to blows, the Italians were heavily defeated at Adowa in 1896, and signed a treaty in that year, which recognized the independence of Abyssinia. This put an end to the ambitious Italian scheme for linking up inland Eritrea on the Red Sea with Italian Somaliland on the Indian Ocean. There followed a series of treaties defining the Italian,

French, and British boundaries with Abyssinia and—to look beyond 1904—in 1906 these three powers jointly guaranteed Abyssinian independence.

On the eastern side of Africa, as indeed in Africa generally, these years were years of consolidating claims, and of defining and usually modifying the inland boundaries, which became more difficult as they were carried farther inland and as they were discovered to be in conflict with geographical facts. In the British sphere in East Africa the Imperial British East Africa Company came to an end, British East Africa and Uganda became protectorates directly under the British Crown, and what was known as the Uganda Railway was constructed from Mombasa to the Victoria Lake. In South Africa Great Britain carried her control of the east coast right up to the Portuguese boundary and inland the Boer republics disappeared, as a result of the South African War. On the western side, Spanish Guinea or Muni became defined by a Franco-Spanish Convention of 1900, whereby France and Spain came to an understanding both as to Spanish Guinea and as to the more northern Spanish protectorate of the Rio de Oro; France secured the right of preemption in both places. Northward from and including the Cameroons, the boundary questions became peculiarly difficult of adjustment, and the boundary conventions were many. It was in the Niger regions and the Gulf of Guinea that the three great powers, Germany, France, and Great Britain, all three converging in Lake Chad, met and collided most. The configuration of Africa in the Gulf of Guinea added to the difficulty. The boundary lines had to be drawn both north and south and east and west. The power that gained most in actual territory was undoubtedly France. She consolidated her coastline. On the Slave Coast she conquered and absorbed Dahomey. On the Ivory Coast she finally closed up all the gap between the Gold Coast and Liberia. On all her sections of the coast she pressed inland and at the same time came down from the north. Thus she secured complete control of the upper and middle Niger, more and more hemming in the other powers, especially the British, and carried her immense empire continuously behind Lake Chad from the Mediterranean to the Congo.

French bitterness against Great Britain culminated at Fashoda and was abundantly shown at the time of the South African War, which followed shortly afterwards. When that war had ended, when King

Edward with his warm sympathy for France had succeeded to Queen Victoria, and while Lord Lansdowne was at the Foreign Office in London, the relations between the two powers began to improve, and eventually, in 1904, the long misunderstanding was laid to rest. On the 8th of April, 1904, a treaty or convention was signed, sometimes known as the Newfoundland Treaty, because Newfoundland figured as prominently in it as Heligoland in the Anglo-German Treaty of 1890. Great Britain gained outside Africa and lost territory in Africa. In return for the surrender of French privileges on the Newfoundland coast, France was given ground on the Gambia and in Nigeria and received the group of small islands known as the Isles de Los, which had been in British possession since 1818 and formed part of the colony of Sierra Leone, though lying to the north of it and over against Konakry in French West Africa. On the same day an equally important joint declaration or agreement was signed whereby Great Britain agreed not to obstruct France in Morocco, and France agreed not to obstruct Great Britain in Egypt. Secret articles, which were made public in 1911, committed each country still further. France and Spain, in the same year, also made a joint declaration as to Morocco and added secret articles, communicated to Great Britain at the time and made public in 1911, which defined the Spanish zones and determined Franco-Spanish relations in Morocco. The published declarations did not infringe the independence of Morocco, but the Secret Articles provided for conditions under which Morocco might not remain independent, and in a contingency France and Spain were assured of the support of Great Britain. The vital importance of the 1904 agreements between France and Great Britain was that the estrangement between these two powers, which had so successfully furthered German designs in Africa, now disappeared, and after 1904 Germany, not Great Britain, suffered isolation. This was, for Germany, a hard fact both to realize and to accept, and it is impossible to resist the conclusion that the clash of European interests in Africa, and the feeling they called forth, were among the determining causes of the War of 1914.

A. J. P. Taylor

BISMARCK'S ACCIDENTAL ACQUISITION OF AFRICAN EMPIRE

Alan John Percival Taylor is one of the most controversial of contemporary English historians and one of the most prolific. His interest in colonial affairs as integral elements of European diplomacy goes back to 1938 when he published the monograph which is excerpted here. An outspoken critic among historians, Taylor presents an interpretation which is provocative yet enticing. The subject is placed in a broader context in his Struggle for Mastery in Europe, 1848–1918 *(Oxford, 1954).*

Thirty years of European concussions came to an end at the Congress of Berlin. In the ensuing period the European powers shrank from European conflicts, and the problems which continued to divide them were, as the French said of Alsace-Lorraine, "reserved for the future." European rivalries were temporarily diverted to the less dangerous field of extra-European expansion, and in the years between 1881 and 1912 the European powers extended their influence or their empires over Africa and large parts of Asia.

This imperialist expansion was of two kinds. The more important was the struggle for the heritage of decaying states, themselves very often the relics of earlier epochs of imperialism. The struggle over the succession to the Turkish empire had gone on since the end of the seventeenth century; but what distinguished the "Age of Imperialism" was that more of these decadent states came into the market and that the process of absorption was rendered more and more difficult by the interference of some other European (and in one case of an Asiatic) power. Thus France was able to establish her control over Tunis, Annam, and Madagascar without serious difficulty; but she extended her influence over Morocco only after coming twice to the brink of war with Germany. Great Britain annexed the Boer republics (relic of an earlier Dutch empire) after a period of conflict with Germany; and she asserted her predominance in Egypt after a period of conflict with France. It was owing to the rivalry of England

Reprinted from A. J. P. Taylor, *Germany's First Bid for Colonies, 1884–1885* (London, 1938), pp. 1–7. Reprinted by permission of St. Martin's Press, Inc., The Macmillan Company of Canada Ltd., Macmillan & Company Ltd., and the author.

and Russia that Persia and Afghanistan preserved their independence —though Persia nearly lost it to Russia in the last years before 1914; and, thanks to the jealousy of all the powers, China preserved her independence, except for the loss of a few ports in what proved to be an abortive partition in 1898. It is not necessary to speculate at length on the reasons for these imperialist activities: the objects of conflict were going concerns; their economic and political importance was known; and in many cases they adjoined possessions or strategic routes of European powers (Morocco on the frontier of Algiers, Egypt and Persia on the route to India, the Boer republics on the frontier of Cape Colony, and so on). The rival powers were still primarily influenced by European considerations; and though the extra-European questions provoked crises, it was the old problem of the Balkans which produced the War of 1914, with the even older problem of the Franco-German frontier as a contributory cause.

The predominance of European considerations is even greater in relation to the second form of European expansion in these thirty years—the occupation of hitherto ownerless territories, or rather of territories with no ruler substantial enough to be treated as an independent power. Under this head come most of Africa and the islands of the Pacific. The enormous areas of tropical Africa appear impressive on the map; but of most of them the plain truth is that they had remained so long ownerless because they were not worth owning. The principal exception was the basin of the Congo, which, curiously enough, slipped through the hands of the two traditional colonial powers, England and France, and was secured by a royal speculator, Leopold II of Belgium, masquerading as a philanthropic society. Portugal, with a shadowy traditional claim to all Africa, managed to retain one colony on the west coast, and one on the east. France, who created a great North African empire within a few years, had intelligible political reasons for doing so: the republican government wished to demonstrate by colonial expansion that France was still a great power despite the humiliations of 1870; part of the expansion was undertaken to protect the frontiers of the existing colony of Algiers; and much of the rest aimed at opening for France an overland route to the Sudan, where—it was commonly believed—it would be possible to divert the upper Nile and so make the English position in Egypt untenable. France regarded Egypt as part of the heritage of

Napoleon, and, in endeavoring to oust the English, was seeking to recover what had once been hers.

England had two interests in Africa, which she meant to preserve— a settlement of British colonists in South Africa, and a predominant influence in Egypt, which was both valuable in itself and a vital point on the route to India. The new English acquisitions were made in order to protect what England already possessed by cutting off the Nile from foreign interference, and the Boer republics, the neighbors of Cape Colony, from foreign help. It is true that these new posses- sions sometimes proved to have a value of their own, such as the diamond mines of Kimberley and the cotton plantations of the Sudan; but it was not for this that they had been undertaken.

In these years of "the scramble for Africa" there was suddenly added to the old colonial rivals, France and England, a power which had hitherto confined itself strictly to the European continent. The German colonial empire, or rather the formulation of its theoretical claims, was virtually the work of a single year: the Cameroons were established in July 1884, German South-West Africa in August, New Guinea in December 1884, and German East Africa was begun in May 1885 (though its frontiers were not settled until 1890); Samoa was added in 1899; otherwise—apart from some minor adjustments of the Cameroons frontier at the expense of France after the second Moroc- can crisis (1911)—the German colonial empire was complete. The success of Germany, as previously of Prussia, had been due to free- dom from all concern in non-German questions: Prussia had been able to secure the support of Russia because of her indifference to the Near East, and of Italy, because of her indifference to the maintenance of the treaty settlement of Europe. It is therefore surprising that Ger- many should have deliberately pushed her way into the hornets' nest of colonial conflicts. The explanation of this German outburst of colonial activity has usually been found in the rising enthusiasm for colonies, and it is true that there was in Germany a certain amount of colonial agitation. Imperial Germany was a "made" state, an artificial reproduction of French nationalism tinged with echoes from the Holy Roman Empire; the new Germany had no political tradition, and had therefore to ape the political traditions of others. Many Germans de- manded a colonial empire simply because other great powers had colonial empires, and their demand was reinforced by the current belief that the possession of colonies was in itself a profitable thing. Many writers, not only German, at this time failed to grasp the truth about the British empire—that it had come into being as the result of British commercial enterprise and industrial success; and they asserted the reverse, that the prosperity and wealth of Great Britain were due to the existence of her empire. The German campaign for colonies rested on the simple dogma—give Germany colonies and the Germans will then be as prosperous as the English.

It is difficult to believe that this primitive outlook was shared by the German government, particularly in the days of Bismarck. It has often been suggested that Bismarck was driven into a policy of colonial expansion against his will. Lord Sanderson, who was a member of the British Foreign Office in 1884, put forward this explanation in a defense of Bismarck written some twenty years later: "Prince Bismarck was personally opposed to German colonization. . . . He therefore encouraged us to make fresh annexations on the west coast of Africa, to which we had been previously indisposed: hoping that the clamor for such annexations by Germany would subside. Suddenly he found that the movement was too strong for him, and that his only expedient, in order to avoid a crushing parliamentary defeat, was to make friends with the party which urged the acquisition of colonies. He went to Lord Ampthill, the British Ambassador, explained his dilemma, said he should have to take up the colonial policy vigorously, and begged that we should give him our support."

To imagine that Bismarck was influenced by public opinion, or that he was swayed by fear of "a crushing parliamentary defeat" is to transfer to Germany the conceptions of constitutional government as practised in England or France. The Imperial German government did not depend upon a parliamentary majority, and the German press was only slightly freer than the press in Russia. There are, of course, plenty of instances—the history of the Schleswig-Holstein affair is full of them—when Bismarck gave the signal for a popular campaign to compel him to do what he wanted to do, but there seems to be no other case in which Bismarck is supposed to have bowed to the force of public opinion. Nor is it conceivable that Bismarck was suddenly converted, after years of scepticism, to a belief in the value of colo-

nies. He was contemptuous enough of those who were ready to disturb the quiet of Europe for the sake of the "sheep-stealers" of the
Balkans. But even Bismarck could not have found words of condem-
nation strong enough for a policy which provoked a quarrel with
Great Britain for the sake of the "light soil" of South-West Africa or
of the head-hunters of New Guinea.

It is the purpose of the following chapters to discover an explanation of Bismarck's colonial policy by fitting it into the structure of
contemporary European politics. His colonial policy alone seems
meaningless and irrational; but when to the relations of England and
Germany are added those of Germany and France, and those of
France and England, Bismarck's policy in 1884 and 1885 becomes as
purposeful as at any other time in his career. Such an examination
shows that Bismarck quarrelled with England in order to draw closer
to France; and that the method of quarrel was the deliberately provocative claim to ownerless lands, in which the German government
had hitherto shown no interest. These lands had a certain negative
value to Great Britain, in that they adjoined existing British colonies
or lay near British strategic routes; but their value was not such as to
provoke the English government into a war. Moreover, they were of
no concern to any other power, and claims to them would not cause
any international complications, such as would have been occasioned
by German demands in China or Persia. The German colonies were
the accidental by-product of an abortive Franco-German entente.

It may be asked whether the later colonial disputes and discussions between England and Germany were similarly related to the
European situation. It would be rash to attempt to discover in German
policy after 1890 any such persistent and successful planning as in
the days of Bismarck, particularly when to the gross incompetence of
his successors were added the planless impulses of William II. Moreover, with the passing of time the German colonies did acquire a
spurious ideological value; they became a white elephant, a sacred
relic of Bismarck's era. He could contemplate passing on their useless burden to England, and even in 1890 the German government
could surrender vast theoretical claims in East Africa in exchange for
the really valuable island of Heligoland. Ten years later the value of
colonies was taken as an axiom by the Germans, and from the failure
of their colonial ventures they drew the moral not that colonies were

a mistaken luxury, but that they ought to have more, and better, colonies. In the first decade of the twentieth century the Germans demanded "a place in the sun"; by this they meant someone else's place in the sun, their own having proved too hot.

Sybil E. Crowe

THE SCRAMBLE AND THE BERLIN WEST AFRICAN CONFERENCE

Sybil Eyre Crowe was a tutor in politics at St. Hilda's College, Oxford, when she undertook the writing of her study on the Berlin West African Conference. Miss Crowe's interest in international affairs was no doubt partially aroused by way of paternal concern. Her father, Sir Eyre Crowe, was one of England's outstanding foreign affairs officers in the early twentieth century and occupied the position of undersecretary of state for foreign affairs. While Miss Crowe insists that hers is a diplomatic history, much light is thrown on African complications as well as on the Berlin West African Conference.

This study is primarily a diplomatic, not a legal one, its object being to set the Berlin West African Conference of 1884–1885 in its true relation to contemporary history. The importance of the conference as a landmark in international law has in fact been exaggerated, for when its regulations are studied it can be seen that they all failed of their purpose. Free trade was to be established in the basin and mouths of the Congo; there was to be free navigation of the Congo and the Niger. Actually highly monopolistic systems of trade were set up in both these regions. The center of Africa was to be internationalized. It became Belgian. Lofty ideals and philanthropic intentions were loudly enunciated by delegates of every country to the conference. Only the vaguest and most unsatisfactory resolutions were passed concerning the internal slave trade, the one humanitarian question of any importance to be discussed at its sittings; while the basin of the

From Sybil E. Crowe, *The Berlin West African Conference, 1884–1885* (London, 1942), pp. 3–7, 11–17, 36–38, 39–40, 47–49. Reprinted by permission of the Royal Commonwealth Society and the author.

Congo, if not of the Niger, became subsequently, as everyone knows, the scene of some of the worst brutalities in colonial history.

As regards the more distant future, it was originally stipulated that the conventional basin of the Congo, a huge area, which, besides the Congo Free State, comprised parts of French Equatorial Africa, of German Cameroons, of Portuguese Angola, of the future British colony of Rhodesia, of Italian Somaliland, and of territories of the Sultan of Zanzibar (which later became British and German East Africa), should be neutralized in time of war. Actually it was found necessary to make neutrality optional. Only the Congo Free State opted for neutrality, and this neutrality was violated by Germany in 1914.

Last but not least, and this is the feature of international law most commonly associated with it, the conference made an attempt to regulate future acquisitions of colonial territory on a legal basis. But here again, its resolutions, when closely scrutinized, are found to be as empty as Pandora's box. In the first place, the rules laid down concerning effective occupation, applied only to the *coasts* of West Africa, which had already nearly all been seized, and which were finally partitioned during the next few years; secondly, even within this limited sphere the guarantees given by the powers amounted to little more than a simple promise to notify the acquisition of any given piece of territory, *after* it had been acquired, surely on every ground a most inadequate piece of legislation.

Important questions of a territorial nature which may have avoided serious conflict, and in this sense made a real contribution to international law, were undoubtedly settled while the conference was sitting. But they were officially outside its program, were not once mentioned during its meetings, and formed no acknowledged contribution to the act which embodied its results. It is true that the conference also facilitated, *after* it had broken up, a series of bilateral agreements made between 1885 and 1886 by powers interested in Africa. These agreements may also have avoided friction, and may therefore also be considered to form a contribution to international law. But they were essentially a continuation of the earlier "ex officio" achievements of the conference, not of its actual work. Besides this they covered a very short span of time, and must not be confused with any far-reaching effect which the conference may have had, even *in-*

directly, on international rivalry in Africa during the next fifty years or so. This appears to have been negligible.

The legal significance of the conference, therefore, *dwindles,* when viewed in true historical perspective. But what, for want of a better term, must be styled its immediate diplomatic and political significance, seems, on the contrary, to grow in importance, the closer it is examined, throwing valuable light on historical problems of the first magnitude, and it is for this reason that it has been chosen as the subject of the present study. . . .

The conference, the first big colonial one in modern times, was held at Berlin between November 15th, 1884, and February 26th, 1885, to discuss outstanding problems connected with West Africa. It was attended by every power in Europe (except Switzerland) as well as by the United States—in all, fourteen powers. Of these fourteen powers only five were of real importance. These were—France, Germany, Great Britain, Portugal, and an ambiguous body called the International Association of the Congo, which had no legal representation there at all, and which was in reality only a cloak to hide the ambitions of Leopold II, King of the Belgians. Its history, therefore, resolves itself principally into the interplay of these five powers. Of these five again, three are more important than the rest. They are France, Germany, and Great Britain. The period under consideration is one in which African and colonial questions generally are still subordinate to European in world diplomacy, colonial issues being more affected by European than European by colonial. Consequently the part played by the *major* European powers is of *major* interest, that of the *minor* ones of *minor* interest.

Among these powers again Germany held the commanding position. Hence the importance of an understanding of the policy of Germany, whose immediate interest in the issues at stake is not always clear. The dominating figure in Europe at the time was Bismarck, and it was Bismarck who held the balance between France and England. Not only was Germany dominant in Europe, she was desirous in Africa, and it is in this combination of circumstances that the *raison d'être* of the conference must be found.

Its history bears an intimate relation to the Anglo-German colonial quarrel of 1884–1885, and its corollary, the Franco-German entente of

the same year (the first and last since 1870), from which the conference sprang. Its conception, it is no exaggeration to say, evolves
literally step by step with the growth of friction between England and
Germany. It is at once the epitome of, and the index to the outcome
of that friction. Each successive stage of Anglo-German tension produced first vague, then ever more determined approaches of Germany
to France. These at first took the form of projects concerned entirely
with a conference on the Congo; they were then extended to the
Niger; then to the general question of effective occupation on the
coasts of West Africa; and finally to an understanding (of which the
acknowledged "Anknüpfungspunkt" was hostility to England) on the
double basis of Egypt and West Africa.

The Anglo-German quarrel of 1884–1885 was not only unfortunate
but unnecessary. This being so, it is to be expected that the history of
the conference should reflect something of its superfluous—perhaps
even its mistaken—nature and this is indeed what it does. Arising out
of a misunderstanding based on false postulates, it is itself an illustration of the mistakes of that misunderstanding. Its diplomatic results
were the exact opposite of what had been contemplated. It was the
fruit of a Franco-German entente directed against England. It resulted
in a weakening of that entente, and, within the charmed walls of the
conference room, though without them the colonial conflict still raged,
of a rapprochement between England and Germany on all the most
important points at issue, it being discovered, when the representatives of the two countries sat down calmly at a conference table to
discuss them, that their interests were practically identical.

This aspect of the conference is of course not the only one of diplomatic significance, but it does seem to be the most important, and
the one of greatest general interest, and will for this reason occupy
the fullest attention here. The part played by Leopold of the Belgians
will take a second place not only because it has hitherto been much
more fully dealt with by historians, but also because it is considered
that this is where it really belongs. By this it is not meant to minimize,
or in any way to overlook, Leopold's role in the history of the conference. He emerged from it, as Bismarck did not, as a real, perhaps its
greatest victor (although this was only realized later). That he did so
was due to the mixture of astuteness and energy, comparable in
quality, though not, by the necessities of the case, in actual power, to

Bismarck's own, with which he succeeded in deceiving all the great powers, including Germany, as to the real nature of his aims. Owing to the skill with which he did this, his sometimes appears as the guiding hand in the very complicated negotiations from which he gained so signal a triumph. Nevertheless his activities were always on a secondary plane.

Ultimately the deciding factor in the whole situation was the general trend of Bismarck's policy, both colonial and European. It was no accident that the conference should have been held at Berlin: no accident either that German restlessness should have been the yeast fermenting the mixed African and European leaven in the years 1884–1885. Germany, at that time, was the arbiter, in a very real sense, of colonial destinies. . . .

The idea of a conference was at first solely concerned with the Congo and only later extended to include other questions. It arose directly out of the breakdown of a treaty signed, but never ratified, between England and Portugal on February 26th, 1884. This treaty, nominally an affair concerning England and Portugal only, actually involved a third power, France, very closely: while in its origin, which must be related to the peculiar conditions prevailing at that time on the Congo, it touched four out of the five powers already mentioned in the introduction to this study, namely—France, Great Britain, Portugal, and the International Association of the Congo.

Portugal was the oldest-established power in the neighborhood, but her claims to any authority in the regions immediately bordering on the river, were of the vaguest, and were not substantiated by any effective administration. Moreover her interests had for four centuries been those of a slave trader, and in 1815 the Congress of Vienna passed a resolution for the suppression of the slave trade. This explains the attitude of the powers when the nineteenth century opens, their complete apathy, namely, with regard to this part of the coast of Africa and their lack of any serious attempt either to dislodge or to confirm Portugal in a position where the only extensive profits to be made came from a trade universally condemned, for which she and she alone was brazen enough to demand special privileges and exemptions.

At the same time, partly to protect whatever small trade of an ordinary nature existed at the mouth of the river, but chiefly to prevent the expansion of a power whose illicit slave traffic was the object of her constant supervision and control, Great Britain, at first in conjunction with France, exercised strong pressure on Portugal to keep her away from it, as well as from both banks and the adjacent coastline, between 5°12′ and 8° South Latitude.

These regions came in this way to constitute a sort of no-man's-land, not owned by any civilized state, where European trade, such as it was, was free to develop under a regime of absolute liberty.

Up to about 1850 the volume of this trade was small. Merchants did not wander much from the coast and they displayed little curiosity as to possible developments inland. About this date however it began to grow. It was discovered that rubber, ivory, palm oil, and groundnuts could be obtained through middlemen from the interior, and that the increased demand for raw materials in Europe, particularly for palm oil, which was used in ships' engines and for sewing machines, as well as for the manufacture of soap and candles, made these products valuable assets in the international market. Big commercial houses began, in consequence, to be established at the mouth of the river. At the same time the activities of explorers in Central Africa were stimulated and increased by the new commercial demands, and it was these activities which finally brought the Congo into the sphere of international interest.

It appears to have been the discoveries of a British explorer, Cameron, who visited the Congo in 1874, after a fruitless search for Livingstone, who had died the year before, and whose offer of the Congo to Great Britain was refused, which were responsible for arousing those budding jealousies on the part of the King of the Belgians, of France, and of Portugal, which were to culminate successively in the formation of the International African Association, the journeys of Stanley and de Brazza on the Congo and the Anglo-Portuguese Treaty. Cameron returned to England in 1875. In 1876 Leopold of the Belgians founded the International African Association at Brussels. This association must not be confused with the International Association of the Congo, which was one of the many subsidiary bodies to be evolved out of it later. It was an association formed by the powers convened by Leopold in 1876 at Brussels, for discussing and devising means of opening up equatorial Africa to European civilization. Its first act was to form an International Commission with an executive committee of four, of which Leopold was elected head, and national committees, which were formally organized between 1876 and 1877, when another conference was called at Brussels to discuss the situation. Great Britain from the first stood aloof from the movement, refusing to form a committee affiliated to the association, and founding instead the Royal Geographical Society in 1877, as an entirely independent body. But Germany, France, Austria-Hungary, Spain, the United States, Italy, Holland, Russia, Switzerland, and Belgium all formed national committees. The important thing to realize about these committees is that they were as jealously nationalistic, probably more so, than if they had never been brought together by an international association, localizing their energies, and appropriating funds accordingly, almost as soon as they had been formed. The foundation of the International Association may in fact be said to have stimulated, not alleviated, as it professed to do, the keenness of international rivalry in Africa.

There is no clearer illustration of this than the story of the rivalry of Stanley and de Brazza on the Congo, between the years 1879 and 1883. Lieut. Savorgan de Brazza (an Italian by birth, but who had long been in the service of the French Government) was the agent of the French national committee of the International African Association; Stanley (English born, but an American citizen), of the "Comité d'Études du Haut Congo," a special body formed by Leopold after Stanley's return from the upper Congo in 1877, to deal exclusively with that region. In 1879 Stanley agreed to undertake an expedition to the Congo as the agent of this committee, and early in the year he left for Africa. But de Brazza, starting a few months earlier for the same destination, succeeded in stealing a march on him by securing, before his arrival, an important stretch of territory on the upper Congo. In 1883, however, de Brazza, who had hurried home to report on his treaties, was in turn forestalled by Stanley, who annexed the valuable districts watered by the Niari Kwilu on the north bank of the Congo.

Both expeditions had been organized with the utmost secrecy. In Belgium the commercial character of the "Comité d'Études" was loudly advertised, its political aims severely concealed, while Leopold kept a tight hold on the press. The political character of de Brazza's mission was also successfully hidden from the public eye in

France. But in fact, the political nature of the program decided upon was responsible for a secret meeting of the French committee shortly before de Brazza left Paris, in which it took steps to establish its national independence, severing all connection with the International African Association, while at the same time more or less affiliating itself to the French Government. Thus de Brazza, when he left France, was in reality in the service of the French Government, not of Leopold's association at all. Stanley's position was even more peculiar. He had, as has been seen, undertaken his expedition under the auspices of the "Comité d'Études du Haut Congo." But on November 17th, 1879, this committee (without Stanley's knowledge) was actually dissolved by Leopold, who took advantage of its financial embarrassments to suggest a kind of voluntary liquidation, in which he played the part of monetary "deus ex machina" and succeeded in placing himself in the legal position of sole director of Stanley's activities. This transaction was naturally kept secret. But in the same month, the name of the "Comité d'Études du Haut Congo" began gradually to be dropped by those connected with it and that of "The International Association of the Congo" substituted in its stead. The transaction once known, it is of course clear in what overwhelming sense Leopold was the driving power behind this newly-titled organization.

It was the territorial acquisitions of de Brazza which were immediately responsible for the Anglo-Portuguese Treaty. This treaty, which was generally considered to establish a veiled British protectorate over the Congo, recognized long-disputed Portuguese claims to the territories lying between 5°12′ and 8° South Latitude, in return for what was considered a low tariff of 10 per cent *ad valorem* on imported goods, and most-favored-nation treatment for British subjects. It also stipulated that an Anglo-Portuguese Commission should be set up on the river, to control its traffic. . . .

There is no doubt that fear of France, and of the exclusive commercial policy of her traders, was the motive power at work in the minds of British statesmen. Already in the seventies French traders had been pushing down towards the Congo from their own colony of Gaboon, and in 1876 the British consul, Hewett, acting under orders from his government, had made a treaty with certain Congo chiefs giving Great Britain most-favored-nation treatment as a safeguard against possible French penetration. Portugal, alarmed for some time now by the increasing interest of European powers in the Congo, was determined to seize this opportunity to extend her rule, at least to the *south* bank of the river, but was still hesitating as to whether she should try to come to an agreement for this purpose with France or with Great Britain.

That she eventually turned to Britain seems to show that she considered her the least territorially ambitious of the two powers—which indeed she was. . . .

It was . . . an African question which caused the rift between England and Germany in 1884, although the relations of the two countries in Africa had hitherto been those of entirely peaceful, though in some places growing commercial competition. There were parts of the west coast, like the Cameroons, where German interests had even outstripped older-established British ones, but in spite of this, British and German traders appear to have been on the most friendly terms. The mere fact that German trade could develop in this way side by side with British, and under the aegis of British authorities, shows of course how little it was hampered by them, and how unnecessary it was that there should be any friction between two countries which were both advocates of the principle of free trade— though it was far otherwise with the French. The Germans themselves seemed to have realized this, for the Hamburg Senate in 1883, in reply to an inquiry of Bismarck's as to what measures they would like to be taken for the more effective protection of their commercial interests on the west coast of Africa, declared that "they had no complaints about districts occupied by the British," though their "traders disliked the treatment they received from the French, especially in the Gaboon."

In any case it was not over the Cameroons, nor any place where keen commercial rivalry existed with England in Africa, nor in fact where it could be said to exist at all, that trouble originated. The Anglo-German estrangement seems to have arisen entirely out of a series of unfortunate, and quite unnecessary misunderstandings connected with Angra Pequena, an insignificant strip of territory on the southwest coast, reputed one of the poorest and most barren in all Africa, whose trifling vaue was quite out of proportion to the storm of controversy which it raised.

After these misunderstandings had occurred, Bismarck proceeded to seize more valuable booty, the Cameroons, Togoland, part of New Guinea in the South Seas (although Germany had hardly set foot in the island before 1884), and later (while the West African Conference was actually sitting), part of future German East Africa. His opposition to the Anglo-Portuguese treaty was an offshoot of the same deliberately anti-English policy, of which these seizures were the result; and the idea of a conference on the Congo (later extended to the Niger and other West African questions), summoned in conjunction with France, was only a further evolution of the same deliberately pursued antagonism to English interests. Its origin, like the other manifestations of his anger against England, can be directly traced to the dispute over Angra Pequena.

Why, it may be asked, should this uninviting and uninteresting piece of territory have aroused passions strong enough to lead to an estrangement between two of the most powerful nations in the world? Germany's interest in the country may be accounted for by the very attributes which would at first sight appear to belie it; namely, its poverty and the savage nature of the tribes dwelling there, which by removing it from the sphere of all serious international rivalry, made it virgin soil for political, as well as economic penetration. . . .

Fundamental misunderstandings arose between the two countries over the whole question, whose immediate cause was accidental, but whose deeper origin must be sought in the British Government's ignorance of the real nature of Bismarck's intentions, the irony of the situation lying in the fact that Bismarck himself was not too sure of them, that he made up his mind to events, as they went along, and that they assumed an anti-English character largely as a result of this ignorance.

At the beginning of 1883, he addressed a demand to the British Government for *British* protection of a *German* settlement made by a certain Herr Lüderitz at Angra Pequena Bay. Only in the event of a refusal did he not claim, but merely "reserve to himself the right" to take it under German protection. The British Government, therefore, had not the slightest suspicion that he ever contemplated such a step. Nor in fact is there any evidence that he originally did so. He lost patience because, after a formal and elaborate repetition of his demand, in December 1883, the British Government kept him waiting six and a half months for an answer, while in the meantime making vague and irritating assertions about their own still unsubstantiated claims to the whole district. This infuriated Bismarck, who meanwhile decided to do what he quite clearly had not intended earlier—namely, annex it himself. . . .

The reason for the British delay was a genuine difficulty with the Cape. The authorities there were willing enough for annexation, but wanted Great Britain to defray the costs. But this was impossible. The situation was further complicated by a change of ministry at Cape Town, in the spring of 1884, which tied the ministers hand and foot, till the elections were over. . . .

It may be questioned whether France in 1884 stood in a potentially closer relationship to Germany than England. On the one hand, a more active understanding certainly existed between France and Germany than between England and Germany, Anglo-Russian tension being a strong deterrent to any close Anglo-German *rapprochement.* On the other must be set the balance of nationalist and patriotic sentiment in France, and the legacies of 1870, rendering any permanent understanding of a close nature with Germany improbable. The odds were about even.

There was no antithesis either for Bismarck between Franco-German and Anglo-German friendship. Indeed, it was largely on account of his understanding with France that he showed himself so anxious to cultivate friendly relations with England, believing that if France, assured as she was of German cooperation in the colonial field, saw no reason to fear English hostility, she would have no incentive to form the coalition, which of all coalitions he most dreaded —one with Russia—Anglo-German friendship being the best bridge for her to this feeling of security. It was to his advantage, therefore, not only to cultivate the goodwill of the two countries on their own account, but to reconcile their interests wherever they conflicted, and this was an additional reason for his support of England in Egypt after 1882, when her military occupation caused difficulties for her with France. He knew that he could win the goodwill of France by other means, but the help which he could afford England in Egypt was as unique for him as it was invaluable for her. Up to the middle of 1884, therefore, he showed himself in every way willing to give it, as well as to do his utmost to bring about a *rapprochement* between England and France.

That he then suddenly reversed his policy must be attributed not to any feature of the international situation, but solely to the misunderstandings which had arisen between him and England over Angra Pequena, leading to further ones concerning his colonial policy as a whole. These misunderstandings brought into play certain features of the German colonial movement, which were inherent in the nature of its growth—an exaggerated interest in any colonial enterprise that offered possibilities of political development, no matter what its real value; an intense susceptibility to colonial propaganda, easily lending itself to diversion against a foreign power; and last but not least Bismarck's own equivocal attitude towards the movement which made his words and his deeds so difficult to reconcile and therefore so mysterious to all around him.

But the immediate cause of the misunderstandings was accidental. They need never have arisen, in the first place, had not Great Britain given Bismarck a unique chance of prematurely beating up colonial opinion in his country by their seven months' delay in answering his simple inquiry about Angra Pequena. . . .

Ronald Robinson and John Gallagher

THE SCRAMBLE: EFFECT OF BRITISH EGYPTIAN POLICY

Ronald Robinson is a Fellow at St. John's College in Cambridge University, and John Gallagher is a Fellow at Trinity College in Cambridge University. Both authors have been intensely interested in the phenomenon of modern imperialism and have attempted to place the outburst of activity at the end of the nineteenth century in broader historical perspective. Their study, Africa and the Victorians, *has been one of the most widely acclaimed and criticized volumes on the subject of imperialism to appear since the end of*

From Ronald Robinson and John Gallagher, with Alice Denny, *Africa and the Victorians: The Climax of Imperialism in the Dark Continent* (New York, 1961), pp. 163–166, 168–174, 175–180, 465–467, 471–472. Reprinted by permission of St. Martin's Press, Inc., The Macmillan Company of Canada Ltd., Macmillan & Company Ltd., and the authors.

World War II. In short, it has already become a classic and will no doubt continue to hold a dominant position in future assessments of the "scramble."

Without the occupation of Egypt, there is no reason to suppose that any international scrambles for Africa, either west or east, would have begun when they did. There seem to have been no fresh social or economic impulses for imperial expansion which would explain why the partition of tropical Africa should have begun in the early 1880s. Gladstone's second administration was totally devoid of imperial ambitions in west Africa. Granville was unimpressed by the dingy annals of the west coast. Kimberley, at the Colonial Office, was eager to give sleeping dogs every chance of lying. The pessimistic Derby, who succeeded him in 1882, was temperamentally opposed to any suggestion, however modest, for expansion on the west coast. Finally there was Gladstone, himself, who knew little and cared little about the problem. In so far as these men possessed any coherent view of the situation in tropical Africa, it was the view sometimes of Cobden, sometimes of Palmerston and the mid-Victorian imperialism of free trade. As in Gladstone's first ministry, they still concurred in looking on tropical Africa as a third-rate adjunct of the British economy, which might be worth the exertion of coastal influence, but did not justify the effort of administration inland. There were none of them likely to plant the flag in the middle of the African bush in a fit of absence of mind.

For decades all the European governments concerned with the coast of Africa both east and west had tacitly agreed not to allow the petty quarrels of their traders and officials to become occasions for empire. The ministries in London and Paris wanted nothing more than to continue their gentleman's agreement, although each faintly suspected the other of wanting to break it. There was little reason for this. Napoleon III had nourished a few sporadic projects for African expansion, but the catastrophe of 1870 had halted them. The Third Republic had pulled out of the Ivory Coast, contemplated renouncing its options in Dahomey, and had hoped to get rid of Gabon and the unpromising claims in the Congo. In Senegal, however, there was a stronger interest. The colonial government there had gradually developed a local expansive power of its own, which derived not so much from its economic potential as from the French army's propie-

tary feeling and its influence in Paris. In 1879 Brière de l'Isle began
the portentous advance from the old colony towards the upper Niger;
two years later the Chambers voted credits for a railway which should
link the Senegal to the Niger. Analysis of this line of policy does not
concern us here, but it had implications for Gladstone's Cabinet. The
rulers of Senegal were extending not only eastwards but southwards.
In 1877 they took a further step towards the encirclement of the
Gambia; in 1881 Brière de l'Isle made a treaty with Fouta-Djalon
which threatened to cut off the hinterland of Sierra Leone; at the
same time private French firms had started to compete for the trade
of the Niger Delta.

To Granville and Kimberley in London, these moves were faintly
disturbing. Poverty-stricken though they were, it would have been
feckless to stand idle while Sierra Leone and the Gambia lost their
hinterlands, and with them, all chance of ever becoming solvent.
Hence the British Cabinet tried to amplify the traditional understanding by a formal agreement. In 1880 they made two separate suggestions to Paris. They proposed that the frontier between the Gold
Coast and the French settlement at Assinie should be delimited; and
secondly that there should be a standstill arrangement between the
two powers to the north of Sierra Leone, to be followed by a commission of demarcation. The French government accepted both these
suggestions. They had to do with regions which in themselves meant
little to the diplomats of the Quai d'Orsay. To their minds it was much
more important to keep in alignment with Great Britain because of
"the interests of our policy in general." The French government
wanted to go into Tunisia and keep in line with London over Egyptian
policy. Obviously, it would go more than half way to meet the wishes
of the Gladstone government in west Africa. The British wishes, for
their part, were plain enough. Best of all, they would have liked to
continue the standstill arrangement along the whole line of coast, so
as to save the hinterlands of Sierra Leone and the Gold Coast for
any future development, and to keep the Deltas of the Congo and
the Niger free from French interference. Unwilling to advance their
own formal authority, their simple ambition was to ward off French
tariffs. All the political problems of the west coast would go on being
shelved; there would be no bidders for its territory; there would
simply be a partition of informal influence. Britain and France could

still both consent to a policy of self-denial. Nobody would annex anything, and furthermore France would promise not to raise any discriminatory tariffs against British trade. Such were the maximum demands of the British. In practice they had to settle for less. A commission of demarcation in 1881 agreed that Britain should not interfere on the coast between the northern frontier of Sierra Leone and the Gambia; while France bound herself to nonintervention between the southern frontier of Sierra Leone and Liberia. The expansion of Senegal had been checked. The Quai d'Orsay could console themselves by recalling that ". . . the British government promised us more cooperation in our other affairs if we regulated the west African question to their satisfaction."

Granville and Kimberley were able to stick to the old ruts of west African policy. The delimitation talks with France in 1881 were based on the assumption that the northeastern hinterland of Sierra Leone was expendable. In the same year Kimberley refused to sanction any step intended to pacify the warring tribes behind Lagos. The following January, the Cabinet had to consider a new offer fudged up by the traders of the Cameroons, and he told Gladstone firmly that "we have already quite enough territory on the west coast." The Colonial Secretary took an equally strong line about the Niger Delta. When Consul Hewett urged that a loose protectorate should be formed between Benin and the Cameroons, Kimberley would not hear of it:

> Such an extensive protectorate as Mr. Hewett recommends would be a most serious addition to our burdens and responsibilities. The coast is pestilential; the natives numerous and unmanageable. The result of a British occupation would be almost certainly wars with the natives, heavy demands upon the British taxpayer. . . .

Looked at commercially, the Niger was the best of a poor lot of trading prospects, and it was worth keeping open to British merchants. But it was not worth the expense of administration. If a protectorate was set up, it would certainly not pay for itself. Moreover, there seemed to be no immediate danger that any other power would rush in where Kimberley feared to enter on tiptoe. True, Galliéni had made a treaty with Segou, and Borgnis-Desbordes was moving on Bamako; but there are more than three thousand kilometers of Niger between Bamako and the Delta. Since 1880 a French firm had been estab-

FIGURE 3. One of the many drawings of the British bombardment of Alexandria in 1882 published by the *Illustrated London News,* this one showing a naval brigade using a Gatling gun. Source: *Illustrated London News,* vol. 81, no. 2256 (July 29, 1882).

lished in the Oil Rivers, but there were plenty of British firms as well. As late as 1882 the British and French governments saw no reason to upset the old coast arrangements for territorial self-denial.

It was the British invasion of Egypt which shattered this system, because it shattered the general Anglo-French collaboration. When

France came out in open opposition to the new regime in Egypt toward the end of 1882, she began to cast around for ways of putting pressure on London. There was plenty of scope for a policy of pinpricks in west Africa, and these now began in earnest. . . .

At the same time, another British sphere looked like slipping away. Trade in the Delta of the Congo was dominated by British firms; in the interior Lieutenant Cameron had made a set of treaties in the seventies which gave the United Kingdom an option on the inner basin of the river. Then Her Majesty's government had rejected it. Now French and Belgian private enterprises were ready to take the Congo seriously. There was a vast river behind the mouths of the Congo, as Stanley had shown; and it had become possible to break into the hinterland, as Brazza had found. King Leopold II of the Belgians, who had floated an International Association to explore central Africa at the end of the seventies, launched Stanley on another mission to open communications between the navigable Congo and Stanley Pool in the interior. At the same time Brazza too went back, acting in the name of the French section of the International Association. Here was a scramble, but only at the personal level of two explorers racing each other to the interior, each with the skimpiest of credentials. Stanley was little more than the personal agent of a petty monarch, for the International Association was a piece of mummery, and the Belgian parliament would have nothing to do with its King's speculations. The status of Brazza was no less peculiar. He too was nominally the agent of the International Association. Although his expedition was given a tiny grant by the French government, the chief inspiration of his mission came from his own pleadings. Paris had little desire to be involved in his adventures. Brazza however had heard that Leopold intended to seize all the interior basin of the Congo, and this would cut off the French colony of Gabon from its hinterland and cast it into bankruptcy. To avoid the ruin of their colony, the French government in 1879 authorized Brazza to make a treaty at Stanley Pool. Just as the Foreign Office in the 1850s had worked to open the Niger hinterland, so the French government in the 1870s worked to open the Congo basin. They were far from wanting to extend their political control into the interior; their aim was simply to block the political extensions of others. Brazza's treaty was meant to "reserve our rights, without engaging the future."

Between 1880 and 1883 Stanley and Brazza played out their game in the Congo. This raised awkward questions for the British government. Leopold was a puny rival, and his association could be pushed into the wings if the need arose. But after Brazza had made his treaty at Stanley Pool, the Foreign Office had to rely on the French disinclination to move in central Africa. In April 1882 the British ambassador in Paris asked the Quai d'Orsay whether the Congo mission had an official character. The discussion that followed showed that in the opinion of the Ministry of Marine and Colonies Brazza had no right to have made a treaty at all. But on the Congo, as on the Niger, all this was to change. After the Egyptian affair had reached its climax, Paris did not feel the old need to pay deference to British susceptibilities; on 10 October the Foreign Minister overrode the protests of the Marine, and announced that he intended to ask the Chamber to approve the treaty. Ratification followed on 30 November. On 15 December the Foreign Office countered by recognizing Portugal's claims to the Congo and its hinterlands—claims which Britain had steadily rejected for the past forty years. In return Britain was to enjoy most-favored-nation treatment in the trade of the Congo, a maximum tariff rate, and the setting up of an Anglo-Portuguese commission to supervise the traffic on the river. The treaty took fifteen months to complete, because the Portuguese went on hoping to get better terms from France than from the United Kingdom; but its purpose was always painfully clear. When it had at last been signed, the French ambassador in London caustically defined it as:

> . . . A security taken by Britain to prevent either France or an international syndicate directed by France from setting foot in the Congo Delta. . . . The British Government . . . would rather parcel it out with Portugal, whom it can influence at will, than leave France with an open door.

That was true enough. During 1883 and 1884 the Gladstone Cabinet hoped to use the Portuguese as a sort of holding company which would decently veil the preeminence of British interests. Lisbon would do the governing, London would do the trade. In fact, British optimism went further than that. It was rumored in the Foreign Office that King Leopold's own organization might become ". . . as I hear is not unlikely, an English company." Both these sanguine hopes are very revealing. As a direct result of the Egyptian occupation, British interests in the Congo were now threatened by Leopold and the French. If their sphere was to be saved, then ministers could no longer rely on the old gentleman's agreement; from now on, official acts of policy would be needed. This they understood. Yet they refused to meet the new situation by any territorial extension of their own. Instead, they fell back on a variant of their technique of informal empire. Others could administer on paper, while they enjoyed the trade. With the King of Portugal as their caretaker on the coast and the King of the Belgians as their manager in the hinterland, all might still be saved, thanks to these regal subordinates.

For all the apparent dexterity of this solution, it was full of difficulties. As negotiations for the treaty with Portugal dragged on in 1883, the French hostility to the project became plainer. In London they badly wanted Egyptian concessions from Paris. Was the Congo worth the cost of rendering those concessions harder to get? Already in May the First Lord of the Admiralty was expressing his doubts to Granville: "I presume we don't want to get into a quarrel with anyone in order to carry out a measure of which the advantage is so doubtful." The Congo was not much of a prize, that was common ground; and from there it was a short step to draw a new conclusion. Since the British position on the west coast was under pressure, ministers would have to resign themselves to the loss of some sphere or other. If the Congo was expendable, then what could be bought with it? Kimberley by June was arguing that the treaty should be scrapped and moreover that the Gambia should be sacrificed, if in return the government could ". . . above all get control of the Niger so as to prevent the possibility of our trade there being interfered with." Now at last ministers were compelled to work out their priorities for the west coast.

But precisely how was the Niger Delta to be kept? In November, a Cabinet committee decided "to establish an efficient Consular staff in the Niger and Oil Rivers District," which should make treaties with the chiefs and induce them to accept British protection. Action to forestall official French encroachment had become urgent. This was the largest possible measure of agreement that could be found in that distracted Cabinet, but it represented the smallest possible measure of official commitment in the threatened region. At most, it meant a wider and a more intensive system of consular rule; but even this was to be whittled down by the caution of ministers. More consuls would mean more salaries; who ought to meet the bill? The traditionally-minded group in the Cabinet were clear that government should not find the money, and the Treasury took the same view. The whole plan was delayed, while efforts were being made to cajole the British firms in the Niger trade to help with the costs. None of them, except Goldie's National African Company, would do so. The outcome of all this shilly-shallying was that not for another six months did the government nerve itself to pay, and Consul Hewett did not sail on his treaty-making mission until 28 May 1884. He was to go down in the folk-lore of the west coast as "Too-late Hewett"; but the real procrastination was that of his masters.

In fact, British plans went astray both in the Niger and in the Congo. Ministers had had their doubts already over the Anglo-Portuguese Treaty. They were to end by thoroughly repenting of it. Although the treaty had been designed to guarantee the interests of British traders, they were loud in opposition to it, because of the nominal Portuguese control and the actual Portuguese tariff. Their protests were joined by the ancestral voices of the Anti-Slavery Society and the Baptist Union. Behind all this agitation there may have lain, as Granville suspected, the fine hand of King Leopold. The complaints of these pressure groups however were not enough to stop the treaty. That it failed was another of the consequences of the Egyptian crisis. After the occupation of Cairo, it seemed to French observers that Britain was driving for African empire. French diplomacy attacked the Anglo-Portuguese arrangement, both as a way of keeping the Congo open, and of putting pressure on the British in Egypt. The treaty was signed on 26 February 1884, and during March the Quai d'Orsay was actively inciting opposition in Belgium, Holland and the United States, the powers with trading interests in the Congo. But in his search for supporters Ferry hooked a bigger fish than these. On 31 March he tried to get the Germans to join the resistance. This overture was to begin the partition of west Africa.

Bismarck too had his grievances against British policy. To his rooted dislike of Gladstone as a man fit only to chop down trees and make up speeches, he could now add a splenetic indignation at Granville's dawdling. In February 1883 he had enquired whether Britain would be ready to protect the German settlement at Angra Pequena;

in December he repeated the enquiry. But for a further six and a half months the only reply he could get from London was a series of vague observations about British claims in that region. In part the muddle was caused by the objections of the Cape, in part by the British feeling that the colonial politicians had to be listened to, if south Africa was one day to be united around that province. But it was an important muddle. The occupation of Egypt gave Bismarck the chance to deepen the rift between Britain and France and to enter the African game. In March and April of 1884 the Germans took steps to assert their own protectorate over Angra Pequena, but the ambiguity of their statements and the imperceptiveness of Gladstone's ministers (one of whom as late as June did not know where Angra Pequena was) left the British as naively ignorant as ever about where their attitude was taking them. It was beginning to take them a long way. On 5 May Bismarck hinted at this in two messages to London, in which German colonial claims and the question of the Congo were ominously linked. By another in this chain of muddles the messages were not delivered. Thereafter Bismarck swung the weight of Germany behind the Congo revisionists and then against the whole British position in west Africa. On 7 June he let the Foreign Office know that Germany refused to recognize the Anglo-Portuguese Treaty and wanted a conference to settle the Congo question. Granville was too discouraged to press on with ratification, and that was the end of the treaty. But the retreat did not stop there. On 4 August the Germans suggested to the French that they should cooperate over west African questions generally at the impending conference, and at the end of the month the French persuaded their new collaborators to join in an onslaught against the least expendable of the British spheres—the Niger.

By now the whole of the British position along the coast seemed to be in danger. The Germans were established at Angra Pequena; on 5 July they had proclaimed a protectorate over Togoland, and on 14 July another over the Cameroons, where Hewett had indeed been too late. In addition, British designs in the Congo had been blocked, and now, as a final twist of the knife, their control of the lower Niger was being challenged.

What had brought about this rout? Fundamentally, the cause was the British intervention in Egypt and its effects on the European bal-

ance. In the aftermath a resentful France had been driven into repu-
diating the former standstill arrangement throughout west Africa; and
now Germany was enabled to press heavily upon the British government. . . .

By the end of September 1884, Bismarck and Ferry had reached
agreement over the official bases for the west African conference. It
was to regulate the division of Africa by defining the concept of effective occupation, and to discuss the measures needed to assure free
trade in the Congo and liberty of navigation on that river and on the
Niger—issues which brought up the whole question of jurisdiction in
those regions. In October, Granville accepted an invitation to the
conference, but in doing so he specifically objected to any form of
international control over the lower Niger. Routed elsewhere along
the coast, he was at last beginning to defend the British sphere in the
Delta.

In July Consul Hewett had reached the Niger at last, and he had
started snapping up territory in the Delta by treaties of protectorate
with the chiefs. He hurried on to the Cameroons, but arrived five days
after the German protectorate had been proclaimed on 14 July. From
then until November Hewett carried on in the Delta with his treaty
forms, collecting a strong hand for Granville to play at the conference. His case on the coast and in the Oil Rivers, at any rate, would
be a good one.

But there were others to the rescue as well. This was to be
Goldie's opportunity. If Granville was to claim that British interests
were already supreme throughout the lower Niger, what of the
French firms operating there, with their treaties and their ambitions
on the Benue? By the autumn of 1884 they were reporting that their
stations had been pushed four hundred miles up the Niger, and five
hundred miles up the Benue. The French companies posed a problem
insoluble at government level. If they could not be driven out, they
might be bought out. Goldie had waged a violent price war against
the *Compagnie du Sénégal* and the *Société française de l'Afrique
Equatoriale* since 1880. The inland trade needed a monopoly to make
it solvent. By October 1884, as the diplomats prepared to settle the
fate of the Niger, Goldie had bought out the *Compagnie du Sénégal*
and was negotiating for the other company. Shareholders of the
Société française were tired of trading at a loss, and they sold out

shortly afterwards. Goldie was monopolizing the river traffic once more, and his agents made a series of treaties with the riverain chiefs. He next turned to monopolizing the trade of the Moslem emirates far beyond the confluence. At the end of December he induced Joseph Thomson, the celebrated explorer, to undertake the task. While the conference was sitting at Berlin, Thomson was moving through northern Nigeria, making treaties for the National African Company in Sokoto and Gandu. Goldie had moved quickly and done much. Whether the French threat to the lower Niger was ever as great as he liked to claim is doubtful; but his enterprise had considerably strengthened the British thesis at Berlin.

With this collection of treaties, purchases and promissory notes, the British government struggled to hold its sphere on the Niger. All this zeal in the manufacturing of evidence was rewarded in Berlin. A timely swing towards the British position by Bismarck, who had little wish to go to extremes with his Francophil policy, and the prudent concession of the Congo, enabled the Foreign Office to make good their claims to the lower Niger. By 1 December they had managed to lay the bogey of an international status for the river. The conference went on to frame a definition of effective occupation, so admirably vague that it mollified the Gladstonians' dislike of extended claims in west Africa. While the Congo basin was divided between Portugal, France and the International Association, the navigation of the upper Niger was placed under French, and that of the lower Niger under British control. It remained for the Foreign Office to decide how its new responsibilities were to be carried out. The critical period was over. At the onset of the scramble, ministers had been almost swept off their feet; under pressure they had at last been forced to determine their piorities. They had staked their claims, they had underwritten their bids, and at Berlin they had got their way.

Why, amid their general retreat along the west coast, had ministers decided to hold the lower Niger? Here was the region with the best trade. Here was the best waterway into the interior. Here lay the best opportunity of breaking the power of the African middlemen. In so far as British policy during the west African scramble was governed by any clear motive, it was to protect trade.

Yet the motives were very different from those postulated in the theory of economic imperialism. It was not the case that the merchants pressed the Crown to pacify and develop the lower Niger for them. Most of the traders still wanted to operate in a *res nullius,* where there would be a fair field and no tariffs, without an imperial authority to tax them and get in their way. All they asked for was protection against the interference of foreign governments and help in breaking the power of the middlemen. Neither was it the case that industrialists and investors at home looked on west Africa as the remedy for their difficulties during the Great Depression. Nor had government when it claimed the Niger the slightest intention of employing the power of the state to administer and exploit it. Indeed, the traditionalists of the Cabinet acquiesced in the sphere on the Niger because they thought it the one region where merchants could be made to pay the bill. The official program fell a long way short of administering the region or turning it into a colonial estate. There is no sign that British public opinion was hungry for west African territory. In 1884 and 1885 opinion was agitated about the Franchise Bill, anxious about the crisis in Ireland and in Afghanistan, agonized about the fate of Gordon. The scramble for the west coast aroused very little interest. At no time before, during or after the Berlin Conference was there a parliamentary debate about its aims or its results.

It seems then that any attempt to analyze British policy in terms of some one decisive factor breaks down before the facts. There is nothing for it but to approach the problem from another direction. Instead of postulating a single, necessary and sufficient cause of these events, it is well to be less pretentious and to define them as the result of an interplay between nonrecurrent factors in the early 1880s. Government policy in west Africa seems to have evolved as a by-product of three major crises, one in Egypt, another in Europe, a third in the domestic politics of Great Britain, and a minor crisis on the west coast itself.

The Egyptian affair had started off the scramble. It had ended the standstill arrangement in Africa. It had run British policy into a noose held by Bismarck. When Germany's policy swung towards France, the two of them squeezed hard on the British position in west Africa. That position was already susceptible to change, as the bases of tribal societies and economies were eroded by the gradual commercial penetration of the interior. So long as other things stayed equal,

Gladstone's Cabinet thought it could cope with the results of this erosion by making only small adjustments in its traditional policy. But things did not stay equal, and the Egyptian aftermath shifted the European balance, blowing these calculations sky-high.

This left the Cabinet in a dilemma. On a rational view of priorities, it was sensible to give ground in such places as Angra Pequena, Togoland, New Guinea, Samoa, the Congo and the Cameroons, so as to hold ground in Egypt. But this involved some political friction at home. During the nineteenth century the political nation was seldom interested in the expansion of British frontiers, but opinion in general, and vested interests in particular, were usually averse to the contraction of their trading empire.

The Liberal administration had come a long way since the glad, confident morning of 1880. By now the Whigs and the Radicals were at each others' throats, and their quarrels had riven the Cabinet apart. The Egyptian misfortunes and Parnellite maneuvers had brought its prestige so low that in March the government was beaten by seventeen votes. From February until December 1884 the government was pushing its Franchise Bill through the Commons and then wrestling over its consequences with the Lords. Whig ministers were alarmed at the prospect of Irish peasants with votes, their Radical colleagues were alarmed lest there should not be enough of them. On top of all this friction and intrigue were superimposed the Franco-German entente and Bismarck's bid for colonies. On this issue the forward party in the Cabinet was able to exploit the Cabinet splits to press their policy on the traditionalists who kept their rooted dislike of African adventures. The Radicals, Chamberlain and Dilke, wanted action. For tactical reasons they were both willing to stomach the German irruption into the Cameroons, but they were determined to make a spirited stand somewhere. They could see the political risks of passivity, and anyhow it did not agree with their temperaments. This was the spirit of Chamberlain when he wrote, "I don't give a damn about New Guinea and I am not afraid of German colonization, but I don't like being cheeked by Bismarck or anyone else"; and by Dilke when he blamed ministerial dawdling for letting the Germans into the Cameroons. But it was not only the Radicals who wanted to do something in west Africa. Granville himself came to think that the lower Niger must be safeguarded, if need be by the extension of official control. Even so orthodox a Whig as the Lord Chancellor, Selborne, wrote:

> *I must confess to a feeling of humiliation at the passive part which we have played, and are still playing, under the idea that a breach with Germany, at this juncture, would make our chances of honorable extrication from the Egyptian difficulty even less than they are.*

The restiveness in the Cabinet finally overbore the moderates. It was common knowledge that the right-wing ministers, Hartington, Northbrook and Selborne might split off, and that Chamberlain and Dilke might do the same on the left. Gladstone in the middle might dislike the whole quarrel over these west African affairs, but under pressure from both the dissident groups in his government he had no alternative but to let the spirit blow where it listed. The future of the Delta cut only a small figure amid the many racking dissensions of that government; but the dangers contained in those other dissensions helped to decide the fate of the lower Niger.

It would seem that the claiming of the Niger in 1884 was motivated neither by increased enthusiasm for enlarging the empire nor by more pressing economic need to exploit the region. The incentive to advance here was no stronger than of old. It sprang from a passing concatenation of minor trade rivalries in west Africa with major changes of front by the powers in Europe and the Mediterranean, mainly provoked by British blunders and difficulties in Egypt. The Liberals claimed the lower Niger merely to prevent an existing field of British trade from disappearing behind French tariff walls; and they limited their new commitment to this negative purpose. They had not decided to found an ambitious west African empire. All they had done in the face of French hostility was to make a technical change in the international status of the lower Niger. Henceforward the powers recognized this country as a British sphere, but government still had no serious intention of administering, developing or extending it. . . .

From start to finish the partition of tropical Africa was driven by the persistent crisis in Egypt. When the British entered Egypt on their own, the scramble began; and as long as they stayed in Cairo, it continued until there was no more of Africa left to divide. Since chance and miscalculation had much to do with the way that Britain went into Egypt, it was to some extent an accident that the partition took place when it did. But once it had begun, Britain's over-riding purpose in Africa was security in Egypt, the Mediterranean and the Orient. The achievement of this security became at the same time vital and more difficult, once the occupation of Egypt had increased the tension between the powers and had dragged Africa into their rivalry. In this way the crisis in Egypt set off the scramble, and sustained it until the end of the century.

British advances in tropical Africa have all the appearances of involuntary responses to emergencies arising from the decline of Turkish authority from the Straits to the Nile. These advances were decided by a relatively close official circle. They were largely the work of men striving in more desperate times to keep to the grand conceptions of world policy and the high standards of imperial security inherited from the mid-Victorian preponderance. Their purposes in Africa were usually esoteric; and their actions were usually inspired by notions of the world situation and calculations of its dangers, which were peculiar to the official mind.

So much for the subjective views which swayed the British partitioners. Plainly their preconceptions and purposes were one of the many objective causes of the partition itself. There remain the ultimate questions: how important a cause were these considerations of government? What were the other causes?

The answers are necessarily complicated, because they can be found only in the interplay between government's subjective appreciations and the objective emergencies. The moving causes appear to arise from chains of diverse circumstances in Britain, Europe, the Mediterranean, Asia and Africa itself, which interlocked in a set of unique relationships. These disparate situations, appraised by the official mind as a connected whole, were the products of different historical evolutions, some arising from national growth or decay, others from European expansion stretching as far back as the mercantilist era. All of them were changing at different levels at different speeds. But although their paths were separate, they were destined to cross. There were structural changes taking place in European industry cutting down Britain's lead in commerce. The European balance of power was altering. Not only the emergence of Germany, but the alignment of France with Russia, the century-old opponent of

British expansion, lessened the margins of imperial safety. National and racial feelings in Europe, in Egypt and south Africa were becoming more heated, and liberalism everywhere was on the decline. All these movements played some part in the African drama. But it seems that they were only brought to the point of imperialist action by the idiosyncratic reactions of British statesmen to internal crises in Africa. Along the Mediterranean shores, Muslim states were breaking down under European penetration. In the south, economic growth and colonial expansion were escaping from imperial control. These processes of growth or decay were moving on time scales different from that of the European expansion which was bringing them about.

By 1882 the Egyptian Khedivate had corroded and cracked after decades of European paramountcy. But economic expansion was certainly not the sufficient cause of the occupation. Hitherto, commerce and investment had gone on without the help of outright political control. The thrusts of the industrial economy into Egypt had come to a stop with Ismail's bankruptcy, and little new enterprise was to accompany British control. Although the expanding economy had helped to make a revolutionary situation in Egypt, it was not the moving interest behind the British invasion. Nor does it seem that Anglo-French rivalry or the state of the European balance precipitated the invasion. It was rather the internal nationalist reaction against a decaying government which split Britain from France and switched European rivalries into Africa. . . .

Both the crises of expansion and the official mind which attempted to control them had their origins in an historical process which had begun to unfold long before the partition of Africa began. That movement was not the manifestation of some revolutionary urge to empire. Its deeper causes do not lie in the last two decades of the century. The British advance, at least, was not an isolated African episode. It was the climax of a longer process of growth and decay in Africa. The new African empire was improvised by the official mind, as events made nonsense of its old historiography and hustled government into strange deviations from old lines of policy. In the widest sense, it was an off-shoot of the total processes of British expansion throughout the world and throughout the century.

How large then does the new African empire bulk in this setting? There are good reasons for regarding the mid-Victorian period as the golden age of British expansion, and the late-Victorian as an age which saw the beginnings of contraction and decline. The Palmerstonians were no more "anti-imperialist" than their successors, though they were more often able to achieve their purposes informally; and the late-Victorians were no more "imperialist" than their predecessors, though they were driven to extend imperial claims more often. To label them thus is to ignore the fact that whatever their method, they were both of set purpose engineering the expansion of Britain. Both preferred to promote trade and security without the expense of empire; but neither shrank from forward policies wherever they seemed necessary.

But their circumstances were very different. During the first three-quarters of the century, Britain enjoyed an almost effortless supremacy in the world outside Europe, thanks to her sea power and her industrial strength, and because she had little foreign rivalry to face. Thus Canning and Palmerston had a very wide freedom of action. On the one hand, they had little need to bring economically valueless regions such as tropical Africa into their formal empire for the sake of strategic security; and on the other, they were free to extend their influence and power to develop those regions best suited to contribute to Britain's strength. Until the 1880s, British political expansion had been positive, in the sense that it went on bringing valuable areas into her orbit. That of the late-Victorians in the so-called "Age of Imperialism" was by comparison negative, both in purpose and achievement. It was largely concerned with defending the maturing inheritance of the mid-Victorian imperialism of free trade, not with opening fresh fields of substantial importance to the economy. Whereas the earlier Victorians could afford to concentrate on the extension of free trade, their successors were compelled to look above all to the preservation of what they held, since they were coming to suspect that Britain's power was not what it once had been. The early Victorians had been playing from strength. The supremacy they had built in the world had been the work of confidence and faith in the future. The African empire of their successors was the product of fear lest this great heritage should be lost in the time of troubles ahead.

Because it went far ahead of commercial expansion and imperial ambition, because its aims were essentially defensive and strategic, the movement into Africa remained superficial. The partition of tropical Africa might seem impressive on the wall maps of the Foreign Office. Yet it was at the time an empty and theoretical expansion. That British governments before 1900 did very little to pacify, administer and develop their spheres of influence and protectorates, shows once again the weakness of any commercial and imperial motives for claiming them. The partition did not accompany, it preceded the invasion of tropical Africa by the trader, the planter and the official. It was the prelude to European occupation; it was not that occupation itself. The sequence illuminates the true nature of the British movement into tropical Africa. So far from commercial expansion requiring the extension of territorial claims, it was the extension of territorial claims which in time required commercial expansion. The arguments of the so-called new imperialism were *ex post facto* justifications of advances, they were not the original reasons for making them. Ministers had publicly justified their improvisations in tropical Africa with appeals to imperial sentiment and promises of African progress. After 1900, something had to be done to fulfill these aspirations, when the spheres allotted on the map had to be made good on the ground. The same fabulous artificers who had galvanized America, Australia and Asia, had come to the last continent. . . .

Jean Stengers

THE SCRAMBLE: EFFECT OF FRENCH AFRICAN ACTIVITY

Jean Stengers is professor of history at the Free University of Brussels and is one of the outstanding Belgian students of modern imperialism. His chief scholarly work has centered on Belgian activity in the Congo, but in his review of Africa and the Victorians, *he offers his own interesting explanation of the "scramble." In suggesting the significance of French activity, M.*

From Jean Stengers, "L'Impérialisme colonial de la fin du XIXe siècle: Mythe ou Réalité," *Journal of African History* 3 (1962): 471–490. Used by permission of *The Journal of African History* and Cambridge University Press. Translated by Raymond Betts.

Stengers clearly indicates how and to what extent he is at variance with Robinson and Gallagher.

It was between 1880 and 1885, as the evidence clearly reveals, that the policy of the European powers took a new turn in Africa. Salisbury expressed it thus: "When I left the Foreign Office in 1880, nobody thought about Africa. When I returned to it in 1885, the nations of Europe were almost quarreling with each other as to the various portions of Africa which they could obtain." Between 1880 and 1885, what had been the first steps in Africa south of the Sahara leading to the establishment of political control over new lands, the first movements toward political appropriation in areas until then free?

Was it Leopold II who started it? It might be so imagined through a reading of the text of the first treaty signed by the agents of the expedition that he had sent into Africa. In this treaty—which was published in 1884 by the American Senate, to whom the king had sent it—the political idea was, apparently, in the forefront: the chiefs of Vivi, on the lower Congo ceded to the *Comité d'Etudes* (the institution serving as a screen for the king) the rights of sovereignty over a part of their lands. This occurred on June 13, 1880. If the text were authentic, the political initiative would be striking. Unfortunately, it is not. Leopold II had communicated to the American Senate a falsified document. The authentic treaty of Vivi of June 13, 1880 has been found, and it does not anticipate any abandonment of sovereignty.

At its beginning, the venture of Leopold II in Africa was not of a political nature. This does not mean that the king from time to time did not envisage or toy with political projects; but these remained in the condition of flimsy projects. The motivating idea, the program —in the correct sense of the word—of Leopold II was found elsewhere. It consisted in organizing the commercial exploitation of Central Africa. To establish trading posts, to set up a large commercial enterprise, this was the first objective of Leopold II.

It was only in 1882 that he was forced to change course, to impose on his enterprise a new direction. He had to face a danger—Brazza. Did not Brazza plant the French flag in the regions of the Congo where Leopold wished to penetrate, even in those areas where the stations of the *Comité d'Etudes* were already established? In order to stop Brazza and to impede his annexations, the only means available was that of planting another flag ahead of his, and one that was also the emblem of a political power. Henceforth, Leopold II looked to acquire sovereignty; moves toward the creation of the Congo State began.

But all of this, which began in 1882, was but a consequence of the policy of Brazza, the intentions attributed to Brazza. In our search for the first initiatives, should we not turn directly towards France?

In truth, it was from France, we believe, that emanated what ought to be considered the two true initiatives in the scramble. The first was the conclusion of the Brazza-Makoko treaty and, even more, its ratification in 1882. The second was the policy of protectorate inaugurated in West Africa in January 1883. The first episode is quite well known, although the reasons for which France established herself in the Congo have never been sufficiently analyzed. The second, we believe, has never been singled out.

In 1882, Brazza returned to France. He brought back what he himself called and what everyone soon called his "treaty" with Makoko. It consisted in fact of two acts in a rather bizarre juridical form— which were manifestly not the work of a specialist in international law —and which dated from September–October 1880. The explorer declared in the first act that he had obtained from King Makoko, sovereign ruling north of Stanley Pool, the "cession of his territory to France," Makoko affixing his "sign" on this declaration. In the second, he declared that he occupied in the name of France a part of this territory situated on the edges of Stanley Pool (that is, what became Brazzaville). This "treaty," to again use the term of Brazza, placed France on a very small territory, of which the strategic and commercial importance at the head of the navigable portion of the Congo was great, but which was isolated from the coast as well as from existing French possessions by hundreds of kilometers.

But how many French, British and other officers had signed treaties of this sort—a little unusual but very adventuresome—in Africa in the nineteenth century, which they had proudly brought back to Europe and which the metropolitan authorities had, with a smile, let lapse? Had not Cameron, to take one example, drawn up in Central Africa in December 1874, a solemn agreement by which he took possession of the Congo basin in the name of the Queen of England? One bureaucrat at the Foreign Office was led to observe that the views of Lieutenant Cameron were interesting but "are not destined to be carried out in our generation," after which the solemn agreement, without further formalities, was added to others in the file.

Did not Brazza risk encountering the common misfortune of so many of the officers deemed too bold by the home country? This he feared and was afraid his "treaty" would not be ratified. In September 1882, in a visit to Brussels, he made some pessimistic remarks to Lambermont, secretary general of the Ministry of Foreign Affairs. He commented that "in his opinion, neither the government nor the parliament would do anything in Paris." From his side, Leopold II, who considered Brazza a dangerous rival among all, used his influence to dissuade France from doing anything about the famous treaty. If the ideas of Brazza carry, he wrote to Ferdinand de Lesseps,

> I am afraid that he will launch his country on the way of annexations and conquests which will infallibly lead other nations to seize other parts of the Congo, to seek also to monopolize a trade today open to everyone. This will be the end of our efforts, the introduction of politics into Africa. The field which we would like to open will be found suddenly closed. Instead of having achieved a great objective of civilization and humanity [understood, the goal that Leopold II himself announced he would follow] to have lifted for the world the barriers of Africa, we will see transplanted there the rivalries and miseries of elsewhere.

Indeed, in Paris the minister concerned, that is the Minister of Marine, was already to enter the Brazza affair. After having stated in July 1882 that he stood "apart" from the arrangements concluded by Brazza, he adopted what administratively constituted the most efficacious attitude for producing nothing: he maintained complete silence.

And yet on October 12, Lesseps answered Leopold II. He had seen Duclerc, president of the Council and minister of Foreign Affairs, who announced to him, he said, his intention to submit the Brazza-Makoko treaty to parliament for approval.

What had happened? The government had decided to act because the French press was agitated. Brazza, with the aid of some friends, had got started a remarkable public relations service with the papers and the organs of opinion. He had amply communicated to the press the account of his explorations, reports on the advantages that his treaty obtained for France, and reports on the immense economic perspectives which would open in a new colony: the French Congo.

From the second half of September, the papers responded, one after the other, to his eloquent appeals. One after the other, they came out enthusiastically for the exploits of Brazza, for his treaty with Makoko, for the French Congo. . . .

In this enthusiasm it is easy to discern the major, dominating part played by national amour-propre. Everywhere it was sensed. A competition had begun in Africa between two rivals: Brazza and Stanley. France upheld her champion and wished him to triumph. Stanley, back in Europe in 1882, attacked Brazza, and declared that the treaty with Makoko was worthless. This became an additional reason for which French opinion rallied around the man who carried its colors.

By making the cause of Brazza in the Congo triumph, by winning this victory for France, one got back at England at the same time. It is here that we encounter again the question of Egypt—but from an angle, it must be underlined, not observed by Robinson and Gallagher. After the indignation, indeed humility that the occupation of Egypt caused, French opinion instinctively sought a means of compensating for the British success. A French success was necessary: the Congo appeared at the right moment. It is for us, wrote a Parisian journal, "the best and surest revenge" for "the mortification" that we recently underwent. Brazza clearly did not hesitate to play upon this sentiment. "An orator who preceded me," he declared during a ceremony at the Sorbonne, "said that the Englishman has got ahead of us everywhere. However, there is one spot where we have set foot before him: the Congo [*Prolonged applause,* notes the official account]. The French flag flies above this land and Parliament has only to say the word for it to be ours forever."

The psychological relationship between the Congo and Egypt, noted by diverse observers, caused the correspondent of the *Kolnische Zeitung,* a person of incisive intelligence, to say at the moment of the vote on the treaty by the Chamber: "The matter has been considered as a work of pure patriotism. Having been supplanted on the Nile by the English, France wishes to seek compensation by supplanting in turn the Belgians and the Portuguese in the north of the Congo."

The Egyptian question contributed thus in a certain way, and a way of undoubtable importance, to the establishment of France in the Congo.

With the approval of the Brazza-Makoko Treaty in the autumn of 1882, the political appropriation of Central Africa began. It was the decision taken by France which truly led to the commencement of the process of appropriation. . . .

In the Congo, French policy had been more chauvinistic than mercenary, and was dictated more by patriotic exaltation than by a consideration of material matters. In West Africa—where in January 1883 the second French initiative was undertaken—the game was altogether different. It was, without any intervention of public opinion and its excitement, a calculated game designed to promote the interests of national commerce.

Commercial interests and territorial occupation had more than one time been linked on the west coast in the nineteenth century. However, this had always been for limited occupation, answering above all to preoccupations of a local or regional order. The last of these maneuvers of a local order, effected "in order to uphold national commerce," had been the creation in 1882 of the French protectorate over Porto Novo.

In January 1883 the plans apparently were enlarged. From the Ministry of Marine and Colonies at Paris were emitted texts which, when brought together, defined a new policy, and that which one is tempted to call this time a grand plan. Successively on the 19th, 25th and 30th of January 1883, three letters were signed by the minister, Admiral Jauréguiberry, which provided a new tone. . . .

Protectorate on the coast from the Gold Coast to Dahomey, political treaties on the Benue, conventions with the chiefs in the eastern delta of the Niger, eventual protectorates at Bonny, Old Calabar or, in this region, treaties in the south of the estuary of the Cameroon. One will see that there is in these texts of January 1883, a political program of scope.

By what men had it been elaborated? Under what influences? What had been the personal role of Jauréguiberry? Had the commercial houses whose interests were involved—and notably the large Marseille commercial houses—taken a direct part in the elaboration of these plans? So many questions to which the files until now have furnished no reply. This is the secret, still not revealed, of the offices of the Ministry of the Marine from 1882 to 1883.

What is in any case clear is that the marine had obtained, apparently without difficulty, the adherence of the Quai d'Orsay to at least a part of its plans. On the letter of January 25, 1883, relative to the Niger and Benue, one finds in the hand of a responsible bureaucrat of the Quai d'Orsay, the annotation: "Write to this effect to M. Mattei" (Mattei being the French consular agent at the Brass River). On March 6, 1883, telegraphic instructions were sent to Mattei.

While the plans were considerable, the means of realizing them were mediocre and, on the whole, the policy defined in January 1883 only produced extremely meager results.

To the west of Dahomey, action was reduced to next to nothing. It was essentially deferred for fear of diplomatic complications. Further to the east, in the Niger and the Cameroons, those who tried with reduced means to execute the new policy achieved very little success.

The first to appear in these regions was an officer of the navy, Godin, commanding the dispatch boat *Voltigeur,* who was charged with carrying out the instructions of January. In March 1883, Godin went ashore at Bonny, the chiefs of which had formerly signed a treaty of commerce and friendship with France. Could this convention be transformed into a treaty of protectorate? Godin immediately realized that "it could not be so imagined."

> How and with what right ask for a protectorate over a country where there are eight English commercial houses, two great steamship companies and where the commercial activity is such that in eleven days, I counted ten steamships enter and nine leave, all under the English flag, while for forty-four years—the age of our treaty—no French commercial establishment bothered to establish itself there?

The commander of the *Voltigeur* thus limited his ambitions to obtaining the renewal of the old treaty of commerce. He couldn't even get this, since the chiefs clearly feared displeasing the British consul.

After this set-back, Godin arrived at the "country of the Cameroons" in April. There also he found English influence established in a predominant manner (to the point, he indicated, that "my pilot was visibly disturbed by what the English consul had said in learning that he was engaged in my service"), but on the banks of the Quaqua stream, which his instructions specially had chosen, he found a "king," the king of Malimba, Passall, who was strongly inclined to sign, and who did sign with no difficulty a treaty by which he ceded half of his territory to France. Such eagerness appeared strange to Godin:

> *How astonished I was over the ease with which he alienated his independence. Passall said to me: I have great difficulty in governing; when you are here I will no longer bother myself with anything but will sleep all day long.*

Passall, whose English name signified that his power surpassed that of all his neighbors, obviously hardly merited this glorious appellation.

If one adds to this treaty with Passall the renewal of the old treaties with the chiefs of Banoko, this is the extent of the success of the cruise of the *Voltigeur.*

Mattei, a little later in the year 1883, had even less success. On the Brass River, where he had his consular post, he brought together the local chiefs in August and submitted to them a treaty placing "their country and its dependencies as well as all their subjects under the protection and suzerainty of France." After a momentarily favorable reaction (for the chiefs no doubt wondered if they might not be able to play France against the English company of Goldie, whose competition they found harmful), the refusal was clear; England was too strong. Mattei afterwards arrived at the middle Niger and at Benue, where he was a little more fortunate, but from a commercial point of view (he was also the general agent of the Compagnie de commerce française de l'Afrique equatoriale) and not politically. It was the same thing at Ibi, far up the Benue where he was able to obtain a concession from the emir of Djebou, before the English merchants, a "site to serve as a market"; this was not, however, a political agreement.

Between the plan laid out on paper in January 1883 and its realization on the scene, there was thus a world of difference. The little that the French did do was however sufficient—as had been the approval of the Brazza-Makoko Treaty in Central Africa—to unleash the scramble. There is no doubt of this for anyone who has looked at the English documents. It was the French initiatives which, grouped together by the Foreign Office and Colonial Office, were at the origin of the decision to act taken by the British government. . . .

In analyzing the events of 1882–1883, we see revealed the new face of imperialism, which it acquired at this time and retained until the

end of the partition of the still free lands of the world. Three characteristics stand out particularly clearly: the development of colonial
chauvinism; the new type of occupation realized with the goal of economic protection in mind; finally, the role of public opinion.

National pride, national amour-propre, and chauvinism all streamed
into colonial affairs with a force they never previously had. In this
respect, Brazza appeared as the great initiator. His propaganda of
1882 no doubt utilized numerous economic arguments; it indicated to
France the direction of rich and fertile lands. But Brazza would never
have been so acclaimed if he had not waved in a moral sense the
national flag. It was when he evoked the tricolor emblem which he
had let fly over the heart of Africa that he seized and led his listeners,
that he carried away the country. Even the economists who subscribed to his views did so more as patriots than an economists. Leopold II, great admirer of Paul Leroy-Beaulieu, noted sadly that "chauvinism apparently possessed" the eminent author of the *Colonisation
chez les peuples modernes.*

In the regulation of African questions, the prestige of each country
—and not only its interests—henceforth entered into account. At the
end of 1884, negotiations were undertaken at Berlin between the ambassador of France and the representatives of the International Association of the Congo, alias Leopold II. There were territorial litigations
to settle. A matter of the frontier? Also a matter of prestige, explained
Jules Ferry to the French ambassador:

> *Even the most doubtful opinion will approve of the Berlin arrangements
> on one condition: that they do not lead indirectly to a victory of the
> Association over M. de Brazza. M. de Brazza is popular; he has a large
> following; he has been entrusted with the national honor. An arrangement
> is necessary which will please the amour-propre of the French people.*

Here is the new aspect of colonial policy; it satisfies a need for
grandeur which, in more than one instance, went far beyond considerations of material interests. In 1885 Yves Guyet, shocked from his
mental habits as a traditional economist used to calm calculations in
all things, wrote with respect to the psychological evolution of his
compatriots, and particularly their attitude vis-à-vis the British colonial empire:

> *We are envious of this vast domain, and we wish at all price to have a similar one with which to oppose it. We no longer calculate; we only listen to passion. We want annexations of which we only see the extent without inquiring about the quality.*

In virtue of the opinion it has of itself, a large country must extend overseas. It thus proves itself to itself and demonstrates to others its national vigor. "Man glaubte," said the German chancellor in 1890, "wenn wir nur Kolonien hatten, und kauften einen Atlas und da malten wir Afrika blau an, dann waren wir grosse Leute geworden."[1] Not to act or to expand, this was to give oneself the warrant of incapacity, prelude to political decadence. Jules Ferry so proclaimed in 1885:

> *It is necessary that our country be prepared to do what all the others do, and since the policy of colonial expansion is the dominant driving force which is carrying away all the European powers we must play our part. Otherwise what will happen will be that which has occurred to other nations which played a very great role three centuries ago and which find themselves today, regardless of how powerful and great they were, fallen to the third or fourth rank.*

"Rank": it was their rank—an absolutely new fact of which one finds no indication before—that the European nations were to defend in the overseas partitions.

This was especially so in the partition of Africa. There, more than in Asia or Oceania, the stakes were clear and well defined: it was a continent that was being carved up. The success of each one was visibly measurable on the map. "In the partition," declared the *Comité de l'Afrique Française,* "France has the right to the largest portion." And in seeking to achieve this goal, the majority of those who supported the work of the *Comité*—the school students, for instance, or the officers whom one finds so numerous among its subscribers—evidently dreamed above all of national grandeur.

In the race which took place economic preoccupations were surely present, but they very often changed their character with respect to those of the preceding age. In the period which, when he retrospectively recalled it, Jules Ferry rightly described as that of "modest

---

[1] "One believes that if we only had colonies, bought an Atlas and colored Africa blue, we would then become a great people."—Ed.

annexations, of small actions, of bourgeois and parsimonious conquests," one had sought more than once to obtain economic advantages and to better the national commercial situation by a well-planned
annexation. These were classical, traditional objectives. The French
commercial houses on the west coast pushed for annexations; they
wanted to obtain a privileged position. The British Counsel on the
Gulf of Benin, Hewett, recommended a policy of protectorate. Such,
in his eyes, would have been above all the means to stimulate national commerce through the establishment of direct commercial relations with the hinterland. Calculations of this sort had a positive
character. In place of positive calculation, soon after 1882–1883
would be often substituted fear, fear above all of annexations by
someone else. One conquered by right of protection, in order to
shelter a region considered menaced by the intervention of another
power which might make its own economic interests prevail there.
The "tariffs" of others: there is, on the economic level, the major ob-
session which struck the imagination.

In the program of the French Ministry of the Marine of January
1883, one evoked the peril of English duties against which it was
necessary to take measures. But the positive aspect was still dominant in this aggressive political and economic program. The English
reply was essentially defensive; annexation was unenthusiastically
undertaken because it was indispensable to forestall the French. By
pushing the Portuguese forward at the mouth of the Congo, England
was equally only defending herself against the French menace:
French tariffs would have been the death of British importations in
this region.

Was a policy of this type truly new? Obviously, there is never complete novelty; precedents are everywhere found. But listen to Gladstone in January 1885 mention "the demands now rife . . . for a system of annexations intended to forestall the colonizing efforts of other
countries." He explained to Queen Victoria:

> *Mr. Gladstone could not honorably suppress the fact that he himself, for*
> *one, is firmly opposed on principle to such a system, and he believes that*
> *herein he is only a humble representative of convictions, which were not*
> *general only but universal among Statesmen of the first thirty years of his*
> *political life.*

When one sees on what scale was about to be practiced the policy which Gladstone considered contrary to traditions—and which was practiced under his very eyes—it is clear that an innovation had really occurred.

There is lastly the third new element: the role of public opinion. In the autumn of 1882, in the affair of Brazza and the Congo, observers were unanimous in insisting that an outburst of the press and public opinion such as no colonial question had ever hitherto excited had taken place. Thus began in colonial affairs a series of public opinion movements at the end of the nineteenth and beginning of the twentieth centuries. It is necessary to speak in the plural, for it is not a question of one of those emotional outbursts, occurring in politics, which literally seize the imagination and dominate it in a lasting fashion. It was by spurts, in a sporadic way, that the flames of colonial enthusiasm moved from one country to another.

However, these flames, which were to spread for nearly thirty years (with the last occurring in Italy a little before the War of 1914), more than once had a real importance in historical development. The example of 1882, which began the series, was one of the most characteristic. Carried away by a nationalistic ardor which surpassed and left far behind economic considerations, French opinion in 1882 practically dictated to the authorities the policy to follow. The government and the Chambers were, according to the expression of the historian Henri Martin, "unable to flinch from the duty which was imposed on them by the unanimous wish of the country." Let's single out this fact and this date. For the first time in the partition of Africa the imperialistic excitement of domestic opinion played a decisive role.

Two years later Germany, in turn, was seized by colonial fever. It was in quasi-clinical terms that those who witnessed it described the phenomenon: "national craving," "colonial mania," "colonial fever," "true fever," "mania for colonial adventure." The excitement reached such a degree that the president of the *Kolonialverein* [Colonial Union] felt it necessary in October 1884 to warn his compatriots against illusions born of an excess of enthusiasm. But Bismarck was a man of a different stamp from Duclerc, president of the French Council in 1882. Despite what the British ambassador to Berlin thought at the time, it seems highly unlikely that Bismarck would have allowed himself to be led by public opinion. His assumed colonial position was a deliberate and shrewd step, analysis of which must be made in terms of high political strategy. But between the policy decided by the chancellor and German public opinion, there was nevertheless a direct connection. One of Bismarck's objectives in entering the colonial domain was doubtlessly to find the theme which would enable him to win the elections of 1884. Once again, there was a major role played by domestic public opinion in this change.

Have the considerations to which we have here devoted ourself a direct bearing on the work by Robinson and Gallagher? *Africa and the Victorians,* in principle, only considers English policy. And does this policy at the end of the nineteenth century confront us to the same extent with the new imperialism whose characteristics we have revealed?

With respect to economic motives, that policy seems to be the very evidence. In 1883–1884, when they began to act in order to jump ahead of France, the British leaders did so by conjuring up, with deep sighs, or, occasionally, anger, the terrible French protectionism that they would not allow to expand. In 1897 Salisbury said to the French ambassador: "If you were not so stubbornly protectionist, you wouldn't find us so hungry for land." Here is found the enduring justification which did not fail to arouse excitement. Sir Edward Grey, in a speech in 1898, described English expansion as having been the chief means of escaping exclusion.

> We had got on the Continent the undeserved reputation of being a jealous, grasping and greedy nation, but the truth was we had been forced into the policy of expansion, because if we had not expanded we should have been excluded. He did not entirely accept the doctrine that trade followed flag, but it had been unfortunately true that where the foreign flag went British trade was certain to be excluded.

Grey exaggerated, but he diagnosed one of the obviously major characteristics of the policy he knew well.

Was "avidity" beyond the realm of British policy? Did England, in its approach to African problems, escape the psychosis of national grandeur, of a place in the sun? There is sufficient evidence to indicate that from a certain moment—incontestably later than in France

or in Germany—this psychosis played a powerful role in public opinion as well as among the men who made the partition. . . .

But did the policy-makers also succumb to the contagion of a
truly imperialistic sentiment? They are presented by Robinson and
Gallagher as reasonable, slow, calculating, and with an indifference,
it would seem, worthy of their predecessors. Were they not carried
along in certain instances by the conquering imagination? One of the
scenes which is lacking in *Africa and the Victorians* is that of the
visit to Hatfield in July 1888 of the young vice-counsel Johnston and
of his conversation with Salisbury, from which emerged a complete
plan for the partition of Africa. All of Africa and its division among the
major powers were suggested on the lawn of Hatfield. In such an instance did not the imperialist dream become integrated into policy?

Furthermore, were the principal authors of the partition—the true
policy-makers—the London statesman, of whom Robinson and Gallagher patiently studied the facts and the actions? Were not those who
took the leadership in the imperialist movement and marked it with
their imprint in London and even more in Africa itself, the Mackin-
nons, the Goldies, the Rhodes, the Johnstons? And among these men
who, more than any others, made imperialism, was there not an evident emotional element? A French diplomat who encountered Cecil
Rhodes in February 1891 was struck by the "sacred fire which ani-
mates him."

> *Last evening I spoke long and informally with M. Cecil Rhodes. He is a*
> *man of forty or forty-five years of age, well-set, with the head and shoulders*
> *of a bull. At first glance, he gives the impression of a brutal force, but one*
> *rapidly perceives that this force is cast in an idea, and that one is facing*
> *more than a businessman, an instrument of government or of a company;*
> *here is the passionate, violent, audacious, indefatigable agent of British*
> *expansion. . . .*

Johnston was also all-consumed by this "sacred fire." These men
made the empire, just as did the French military leaders in West
Africa, often without approval from Paris. And so did Leopold II, who
created his own empire from his palace in Brussels by the endless
repetition of his orders. All did this because they had a passion for
the vast lands they could conquer for their country. . . .

To conclude, once again let us return to Egypt. Would events have occurred as they did in Africa south of the Sahara without the occupation of Egypt? If the Egyptian question had not caused a desire and need for retaliation, would French public opinion have embraced the cause of Brazza as it did? When one is dealing with collective emotional movements, the "What-would-have-happened-if" are—let's face it—nearly always futile questions. There are always too many imponderables in emotion which escape analysis.

But the scramble also had at bottom its economic reasons. And here there is no doubt possible. Egypt or no Egypt, economic factors would have in any case sooner or later started the movement.

The fundamental element that should be in mind is the following: from the moment when the economic penetration of the Dark Continent was begun, the temptation was strong, even irresistible, to reserve in one way or another certain advantages in those regions into which a country penetrated. The march toward the interior was in many instances almost nearly synonymous with the acquisition of economic privileges.

C. W. Newbury and A. S. Kanya-Forstner
FRENCH POLICY AND THE SCRAMBLE

C. W. Newbury of Oxford University and A. S. Kanya-Forstner of Cambridge University are both authors of significant studies of European penetration into West Africa. In this article they offer a most important revisionist thesis which places French activities in West Africa in a new historical perspective. The article has been described as brilliant, and it has been widely recognized as basic to any appreciation of the causal patterns of the scramble for Africa.

The origins of the partition of Africa have been the subject of much debate in recent years. It is generally agreed that the ratification of the de Brazza treaty and a series of French naval and consular initia-

From C. W. Newbury and A. S. Kanya-Forstner, "French Policy and the Origins of the Scramble for West Africa," *Journal of African History* 10 (1969): 253–257, 259–264, 270–275. Used by permission of *The Journal of African History* and the Cambridge University Press.

tives in the Gulf of Guinea sparked off the scramble for West Africa in the winter of 1882–1883. But the motives for this intensification of French activity and the reasons for its apparent suddenness have yet to be satisfactorily explained. In the past, the origins of the scramble have been studied as an episode in the diplomacy of European imperialism. Our aim in this paper is to examine the questions they raise in relation to the dynamics of French expansion. By taking the development of French African policy since the beginning of the nineteenth century as our frame of reference, we hope to show that the initiatives of 1882–1883 were a less radical departure from previous policies than has hitherto been assumed, and that they had more far-reaching implications than has hitherto been suggested.

Considerations of strategy and trade—some would add prestige—governed the African policies of the European powers during the nineteenth century, and France was no exception. To achieve her strategic and commercial objectives in West Africa, she adopted two distinct techniques. On the coast, from the Senegal to the Congo, limited political commitments were the rule. In the early 1840s the threat of British expansion did provoke a French response: the fortified posts at Assinie, Grand Bassam and Gabon were built to combat the growth of British influence, to provide stations for the French navy, and to protect French trade. But they were not intended to serve as springboards for expansion inland. Only external sovereignty was claimed over their sites, and direct interference in local African politics was kept to a minimum. By the 1860s, moreover, the failure of this *politique des points d'appui* could no longer be ignored. The *comptoirs* on the Ivory Coast, poorly situated, weakly defended and unhealthy, were strategically useless; after the reduction of the West African squadron in 1848, even the strategic value of Gabon became more notional than real. Nor could official support do much to further trade when French traders had neither the capital, the experience nor the incentive to compete effectively with their British rivals. Indeed, the most successful commercial house, Régis Frères of Marseille, made its profits without the backing of the state. The most lucrative sector of its activity was the palm-oil trade of the Slave Coast, where the firm operated from an abandoned French fort and relied for protection on the rulers of Dahomey, not on the commandants of the West African naval station. . . .

What gave Senegalese policy after 1840 a new dimension was the French conquest of Algeria. The North African experience of founding empires by military domination, instead of by influence or trade, was quickly translated into West African terms. . . .

The French advance south from Algeria also opened a new route into the West African interior and increased the government's interest in the coveted Sudanese markets. By 1847 Paris was aiming at nothing less than their exclusive commercial and political control. . . .

But this new conception of empire was not as revolutionary as it appeared. As far as the western Sudan was concerned, the policy-makers of the 1850s were still informal imperialists. Since the beginning of the century, their objective had been to exploit the riches of the far interior, to open new outlets for French manufacturers, and so to further "la cause de la civilisation et de l'humanité . . . qui ne peut être mieux servie que par les pacifiques conquêtes du commerce et de l'industrie." The emphasis on political control evident in their Senegalese policy was absent from their calculations; the peaceful extension of trade and influence was the limit of their aspirations. They wanted a loose commercial empire, not a political dominion. And they certainly had no intention of creating this empire by force of arms.

Governor Louis Faidherbe of Senegal was the first to grasp the relevance of the Algerian precedent for the western Sudan. His participation in the conquest of North Africa made him a strong partisan of "une occupation plus sérieuse du Sénégal." Like the Algerian officers, he saw the problem of security as his chief concern and the destruction of all opposition by superior military force as the most effective solution to it. On the Senegal, he crushed the Moors, annexed Walo, and successfully withstood the challenge of the Tokolor leader, al-Hajj 'Umar. His approach to the question of the western Sudan was equally vigorous. Rejecting the cautious pacifism of his metropolitan superiors, he called for a military advance beyond Médine, the destruction of the Tokolor empire, and the construction of a chain of forts to the Niger. These measures, he confidently predicted, would lay the foundations of an empire which might one day rival Canada or India. In 1863 he drew up still more ambitious proposals. France, he now maintained, must establish her undisputed mastery over the "Senegambian triangle" by occupying Bamako on

the Niger and by securing the Gambia in exchange for French possessions on the Guinea coast. From Bamako, the French could send
gunboats to patrol the river as far as Bussa, and then complete their
drive into the Sudan by moving upstream from the delta in concert
with the British. . . .

But Faidherbe's dreams were not to be fulfilled. Although the
Minister of Marine, Chasseloup-Laubat, admitted the attractiveness of
the plan, he doubted whether the Gambia would be worth the sacrifice of Gabon, and he could not see how the Portuguese were to be
compensated for their enclave in Guinea. By 1864, moreover, France
was fully committed in Mexico and Indo-China, and the minister had
neither the money nor the enthusiasm for empire-building in West
Africa. . . .

The disasters of the Franco-Prussian War made any change in the
policy of retrenchment materially impossible. In the aftermath of defeat, all the resources of the state had to be devoted to internal re-
construction, and without money there could be no thought of West
African expansion. Once more, Senegal was relegated to the status
of "un agrégat de comptoirs coloniaux. . . ."

Yet the significance of these early years must not be underesti-
mated; by the 1870s the broad lines of imperial strategy were clear.
On the West African coast, the principle of official support for trade
had been tentatively established. On the lower Senegal, the principle
of political control as the corollary to economic activity had been fully
applied. French interest in the future of the African interior had been
amply demonstrated. Governor Faidherbe had drafted the blueprint
for a Sudanese empire on the Algerian model and had thus planted
the seeds of French imperialism in West Africa. So far, these seeds
had been kept from sprouting by the reluctance of Paris to pay for a
genuinely imperialist program of expansion. In the years after 1876
this reluctance was to be overcome. . . .

The revival of Faidherbe's Niger plan heralded a major change in
French African policy. In 1876, Paris had still been firmly committed
to a policy of consolidation, economy and peace, but Brière[1] soon
demonstrated the metropolitan government's inability to control a determined local subordinate who was astute enough to perceive its

[1] Brière de l'Isle, governor of Senegal, between 1876 and 1881.

weaknesses and bold enough to exploit them. No matter how much ministries may have opposed territorial expansion, they could not permit the establishment of a foreign presence on the upper Niger and they dared not ignore reports of British action there. Whatever their scruples about the use of force, they dared not forbid a military advance when the security of existing French possessions was said to be at stake. And even when they prohibited military action, they could not prevent the *fait accompli;* the Futa campaign had been proof enough of that.

But local initiative was not enough. Brière's plans involved much more than the extension of French influence to the Niger. The construction of a railway through 600 miles of territory, much of it unexplored, entailed a much higher level of expenditure than Paris had so far contemplated. The establishment of the security necessary for railway-building implied a much greater degree of political control than Paris had so far envisaged. If the creation of a West African empire was to become a serious objective of French policy, Paris itself had to make it so.

Historians of French expansion generally dispute the emergence of new themes in official thinking about African questions during the late 1870s. As far as the West African coast is concerned, this interpretation has much to recommend it. The Ministry of Marine and Colonies, and in particular the commanders of the off-shore naval squadrons charged with the defense of French commercial interests, had long been suspicious of the self-interested motives of the coastal traders and had never been anxious to assume major political commitments on their behalf. The Ministry of Foreign Affairs was equally determined not to allow local differences to complicate its general policy of maintaining good relations with Great Britain. Since the 1860s both departments had favored a comprehensive settlement involving a territorial exchange as the most satisfactory solution to petty West African disputes, and this remained their policy even after the failure of the Gambia negotiations in 1876. . . .

On the Senegal, however, conventional arguments about French policy are much more difficult to sustain. Admittedly, the expansionist cause did not arouse much popular enthusiasm in the immediate aftermath of a military disaster which many blamed on Napoleon's overseas adventures. But colonial expansion was not universally unpopular; the members of the burgeoning geographical societies, some intellectuals and publicists, a few aspiring explorers, and several deputies as well, saw it as the one source of their nation's regeneration. Tales of the Sudan's limitless wealth and the old dream of a north-west African empire had obvious attractions for them. Their plans to tap this wealth through railways were equally natural in an age when transcontinental railways were opening up the American West, and when there was talk of a Siberian railway to open up the Russian East. With remarkable persistence and energy, the new colonial enthusiasts published brochures, organized lecture tours and financed exploration of the route for a trans-Sahara railway which was to link Algeria with Senegal and so make their imperial dream come true. Their efforts were not unrewarded. Adolphe Duponchel's *Chemin de fer transsaharien* became a minor best-seller, and in May 1879 Gambetta's young disciple, Paul Bert, proposed a parliamentary vote of 200,000 francs to cover the cost of preliminary surveys. The response of the Chamber could hardly have been more enthusiastic. . . . Six months later both the Chamber and the Senate eagerly voted an additional 600,000 francs for the scheme.

Colonialist propaganda had an effect upon the policy-makers as well. At first agitation for the trans-Sahara railway had made little impact upon the ministries, and requests for financial assistance were generally rejected. But the government was not completely indifferent to the future of the West African interior. In 1877 the Ministry of Public Works gave Duponchel a grant of 4,000 francs as a token of its interest in his work, and when the publication of his report revealed the popularity of his scheme, the minister, Charles de Freycinet, quickly set up a departmental commission to study its feasibility. In July 1879 a full *Commission Supérieure* was convened to study all aspects of the program. Parliament's enthusiastic support for the project, Freycinet admitted, was a major factor in his decision to proceed.

But this change in official policy was not simply a response to the pressures of public opinion. Freycinet himself was a passionate railway-builder who had already set his heart upon transforming the whole French railway system. Since 1877, moreover, his department had been at work on the reorganization of the Algerian railways, and it was just completing its studies when Duponchel's report was published. For the minister and his staff the trans-Sahara was an extension of a still more ambitious program of railway-construction. More significantly, Freycinet was also a passionate expansionist, determined to regain in the colonial sphere the primacy which France had lost in Europe. And in December 1879 Freycinet became prime minister. . . . Freycinet's intentions were clear enough.

So too were those of the Ministry of Marine. In February 1879 Admiral Pothuau had been replaced by Admiral Jean Jauréguiberry, a former governor of Senegal and as ardent an expansionist as Freycinet. Brière's plans for an advance to the Niger were now assured of a more sympathetic reception; within weeks of taking office Jauréguiberry had committed his ministry to a more energetic Sudanese policy. In July Brière was asked for details about the cost of occupying Bafoulabé and building a connecting road to Médine. In September, taking advantage of the parliamentary recess, Jauréguiberry secured a grant of 500,000 francs by presidential decree. When funds ran out, he authorized a further expenditure, again without parliamentary approval. Meanwhile, the minister also approved the Senegal-Niger railway project, and his *inspecteur-général des travaux maritimes,* N. C. Legros, obtained the support of Freycinet's *Commission Supérieure.* By July 1879 the Niger railway had become an integral part of the trans-Sahara railway network.

Freycinet and Jauréguiberry, not the geographical societies or the explorers, were the true architects of the new African policy. The two men were intimate friends and close political allies. They shared a common belief in the Sudan's economic potential and a common determination to exploit it for their nation's benefit. They were convinced that the race for Africa had begun, and that the state, with all the resources at its command, had to make the running. One of them, a technocrat, placed his faith in French technological expertise; the other, a professional soldier, in forts and strategic communications. Together they set out to establish French sway over the major portion of the African interior. . . .

Urged on by the Senegalese administration, influenced by public opinion, but motivated primarily by its own imperial ambitions, the French government had accepted the financial implications of African expansion.

There remained the question of security. The objective of the railway enthusiasts was the traditional one of an informal commercial empire. . . . Freycinet too spoke of "peaceful conquests," as his predecessors had done fifty years before, and he gave his Saharan missions strict orders to keep the peace. But these were not the views of Jauréguiberry. Although he assured Freycinet that his only wish was to "prendre part au mouvement général qui porte les nations européennes à pénétrer au cœur de l'Afrique pour y ouvrir de nouveaux débouchés à leur commerce," his intentions were political rather than economic. The purpose of the railway was to extend French dominion to the Niger; its commercial profitability was a secondary consideration. Although he spoke of the railway's absolutely peaceful character and piously denied any desire to "accroître notre situation militaire dans ces contrées," he was ready to achieve his political objective by military means. By July 1879 his ministry was already considering Faidherbe's old plans for building forts and placing a gunboat on the Niger. When the Budget Commission rejected the railway project and granted only 1.3 million francs for continued surveys, Jauréguiberry used part of the money to pay for an extra battalion of *tirailleurs sénégalais* and a new fort at Kita, halfway between Bafoulabé and the Niger. Finally, in September he placed the Sudan under military command, appointing Major Gustave Borgnis-Desbordes as *Commandant-Supérieur du Haut-Fleuve* with full control over all operations on the upper Senegal. This was the crucial decision. By accepting the political and military implications of an advance to the Niger and by entrusting the execution of his policies to military agents, Jauréguiberry had raised the curtain on the era of French imperialism in West Africa. . . .

What was the significance of these French moves? What were their motives and the reasons for their timing? One cannot answer these questions by concentrating exclusively upon the immediate origins of the scramble for territory which they provoked. The ratification of the de Brazza treaty, for example, was not a crucial turning-point in French expansion as some have pictured it. De Brazza had no official powers to negotiate, and the government was reluctant to accept the results of his unauthorized diplomacy. Jauréguiberry regarded the explorer as a foreign upstart in the pay of a private organization closely linked with King Leopold of the Belgians, and he tacitly opposed the submission of the treaty to parliament. Even after its ratification, both he and the Quai d'Orsay warned their agents: "La question du Congo n'est pas la seule importante. L'obligation de concentrer nos efforts sur d'autres points, la situation d'ensemble de notre empire colonial et les complications qu'elle peut amener vous indiqueront les sages limites que vous ne devez pas dépasser dans un pays où jusqu'ici nos intérêts son relativement faibles."

As is well known, the pressure of public opinion forced the government to act. But the success of the Congo lobby's propaganda campaign and the popular enthusiasm which it aroused did not reveal "le visage neuf de l'impérialisme." De Brazza's supporters had done just as well with their agitation over the trans-Sahara railway three years before, and the reasons for their success were the same in both instances. Parliament ratified the de Brazza treaty because it gave France a new route into the vast and wealthy lands of the West African interior. . . .

The repercussions of the occupation of Egypt also had little significance for French expansion in West Africa. Certainly, the British occupation had a profound effect upon the general course of Anglo-French relations, and it may have facilitated the adoption of more overtly anti-British policies, just as public reaction to the occupation may have contributed to the success of de Brazza's publicity campaign. But Jauréguiberry's protectorate policy was designed to defend French interests in West Africa, not to drive the British out of Egypt. And Anglo-French hostility was no new phenomenon; fears of British expansion had plagued Jauréguiberry ever since he first came to office in 1879. Even the suddenness of the minister's actions in January 1883 can be explained without reference to Egypt. There is strong circumstantial evidence that he and his advisers were forced by domestic considerations to activate their plans while they still had the opportunity. At the time, France was in the grip of a serious ministerial crisis over the proposed expulsion of the princes from the armed forces. Jauréguiberry was violently opposed to the measure, and when the government asked for discretionary powers to deal with individual cases on 19 January, he must have known that his days in the cabinet were numbered. On that same day, his proposals for the occupation of Porto-Novo and the extension of a French protectorate along the Slave Coast were sent to the Quai d'Orsay. His orders to the South Atlantic Naval Division, issued without consulting the Foreign Ministry, were actually signed two days after his resignation and the day before he was finally replaced.

Those who emphasize the commercial factor in French expansion have a much stronger case. The protection of coastal trade had been a prominent theme since the 1870s, and, after the failure to reach a comprehensive settlement, the pressures to assume territorial commitments in its defense became powerful indeed. But coastal trade was not the policy-makers' sole concern. Jauréguiberry himself was much more interested in the future commercial prospects of the interior. The extension of French influence along the Niger-Benue complex was the most important element in his protectorate program. . . . Jauréguiberry's protectorates were not simply an attempt to safeguard the coastal trading interest; they were also part of a two-pronged assault aimed at the creation of a vast territorial empire in the West African interior. Admittedly, this was a long-term and a rather vague objective; the minister himself never described the occupation of Bamako and his plans for the lower Niger as two related elements in a fully developed policy of imperial expansion. But the simultaneous advance on both fronts was clearly more than pure coincidence. Soleillet had talked of such an empire in 1876, and the Colonial Department had noted his views. Rouvier's speeches had echoed the same theme after 1879. Twenty years before them, Faidherbe had drafted detailed plans for the empire's creation, and his were the blueprints which the Ministry of Marine was using.

Certainly, there had been a revolution in French African policy; but one cannot grasp its significance by studying the diplomacy of imperialism, because this revolution preceded the diplomatic phase of the partition. The French entry into the politics of the lower Niger and the Congo was not the start but the continuation of a new policy. By then the fascination of Sudanese wealth, the fear if not the reality of foreign rivalry, and the triumph of protectionist sentiment had already whetted appetites for African territory and rendered the old techniques of informal expansion obsolete. The crucial change in French policy was the transition from informal to formal empire; it took place not in 1882–1883 but in 1879–1880.

What brought this change about? Local crises in Africa cannot provide the complete answer. The breakdown of the traditional pattern of trade along the coast may have forced the French to intervene politically; but even here their objectives were not limited to the protection of existing trade from British competition. And in the western Sudan no growth of African opposition forced them to adopt the techniques of military conquest. Tokolor resistance did not provoke the capture of Murgula or the occupation of Bamako; the fall of Murgula and the loss of Bamako did not even provoke Tokolor resistance. The conquest of the western Sudan was not an involuntary response to the pressure of local African circumstance but a determined European bid for territory.

Developments in French political life can provide only a partial explanation. The stabilization of the republic after the elections of 1877 and 1879 and the resignation of MacMahon, the return of France to the diplomatic stage at the Congress of Berlin, and the new spirit of self-confidence which these developments engendered should all be kept in mind. But they merely provided the back-drop to the process of policy-making. The nationalist and expansionist sentiments of French public opinion are more directly relevant. The popularity of the trans-Sahara railway was one of its most significant characteristics; the popularity of de Brazza was his most powerful weapon. Parliament was sympathetic to all the government's West African schemes. Twenty-five million francs were spent on the Senegal railway before the Chambers finally called a halt, and even the government's sternest critics did not dare to criticize its political objectives or to question the value of its projected African empire. But the impact of public opinion was sporadic and selective, and opinion itself was unstable; the agitation in favor of the trans-Sahara railway and de Brazza was more than matched by the furor over the Tunisian campaign. Nor can sudden bursts of nationalist fervor account for the origins of the policies pursued after 1879. Public opinion may on the whole have supported African expansion; it did not initiate the process.

Pressure from private commercial interests also played its part. Bordeaux merchants, the most influential group in Senegal, had long coveted the trade of the western Sudan. In 1851 and 1854 they campaigned for the appointment of Faidherbe and petitioned the government to open up the river *escales.* In 1879 the firm of Murel et Prom supported the railway scheme; in 1880 it set up shop at Médine; by 1883 it had two steamers plying between Saint-Louis and Kayes.

Along the southern rivers Verminck and his associates tirelessly demanded official protection and support, as did the CFAE [Compagnié française de l'Afrique équatoriale] in the Niger Delta. Governments did not remain deaf to their appeals. But ministers like Jauréguiberry were anything but traders' cat's-paws. They made a clear distinction between the national and the private interest, and it was the former, not the latter which they tried to serve. Nor were the traders empire-builders to a man. They were divided on important issues such as fiscal control and administrative responsibility. Their operations were limited to the coast and the river *escales;* even the Bordeaux merchants on the upper Senegal were more interested in the profits to be had from supplying the expeditionary forces and transporting material for the railway than in gum or gold. And those who saw their trade threatened by the increased competition which the railway would bring, actively opposed and obstructed the government's plans. In France, moreover, the most influential commercial pressure groups, the Bordeaux and Marseille chambers of commerce, lagged far behind the government in their appreciation of Africa's future commercial importance.

Indeed, it was the local Senegalese administration which often stated the commercial arguments most forcefully. Brière de l'Isle was the most insistent in his demands for the revival of mercantilist principles in French African trade, and the most effective in undermining the government's commitment to peace. Once the military advance began, the military themselves became the focus of local initiative. The agents of expansion exerted the pressures which most affected the policy-makers. But French expansion in Africa was more than a case of "a little local imperialism." Senegal alone could not secure the massive capital outlay on which the Niger plan depended. And the decision to introduce the military factor was taken in Paris; Jauréguiberry was the man who sent Desbordes to the Sudan.

Ultimately, the motives for French expansion are to be found within the policy-making framework itself, within the "official mind" of French imperialism. What transformed French policy after 1879 was a change in official thinking on the vital questions of cost and military effort. Freycinet and Jauréguiberry were the ones who broke with the tradition of limited government intervention in African affairs. Alarmed by the imagined threat of foreign competition they made the state the principal agent of African expansion. Convinced of Africa's legendary wealth, they invested public funds in its future profitability. Discarding the old notions of informal empire, they made political control the basis for economic development, and they set out to win their empire by military means. This last was the crucial decision, and for it the Ministry of Marine rather than the Ministry of Foreign Affairs was the department primarily responsible. Within the ministry a group of dedicated and energetic officials—Legros, Dislère and the head of the Upper Senegal Bureau, Lieutenant-Colonel Bourdiaux—provided a strong supporting cast; but, on the evidence available, Jauréguiberry himself seems to have acted the leading part.

French expansion in West Africa had its peculiarities. Its economic objectives were all-important, but these did not derive from any profound changes within the structure of the French economy or even from any serious assessment of Africa's economic potential. The policymakers of the 1880s, like their predecessors of the 1820s and 1830s, fell victim to the myth of Sudanese wealth. Their calculations were no more solidly based than they had been half a century before. Jauréguiberry's estimate of a Sudanese market of 80 million people was hardly the product of careful study, and Jauréguiberry was by no means unique. More intelligent men like Freycinet and more sophisticated economists like Rouvier talked blandly of markets three times the size. When policies are based on myths, they can be as fanciful as the objectives they seek to attain. But this does not make them any the less significant. The age of imperialism was not an Age of Reason, and French policies were nothing if not the product of their age.

Any interpretation of the partition must take this imperialist phenomenon into account. The policies of Freycinet and Jauréguiberry contained the very essence of late-nineteenth-century imperialism; they were the Gallic "doctrine of tropical African estates" enunciated fifteen years before Chamberlain came to office. And this difference in timing was vital. By 1895 the scramble for West Africa was virtually over; in 1880 it had yet to begin. Chamberlain's doctrine may have "inspired the beginnings of . . . modern administration" in Britain's African territories; its French counterpart inspired the actual process of expansion. The beginnings of British imperialism in West Africa may have been a consequence of the partition; the beginnings of French imperialism were its cause.

II THE PROBLEM FROM THE AFRICAN HISTORICAL PERSPECTIVE

Georges Hardy

THE SCRAMBLE: PRECONDITIONS AND POSTCONDITIONS IN AFRICA

Georges Hardy is one of the oldest and most significant authorities of French colonial history; he is, in effect, doyen of them all. As director of the Ecole Coloniale in Paris—the training school for future French colonial administrators—he played an active as well as an academic role in colonial matters. The number of books he has written on French colonial policy is large, and any student of French colonialism owes him a great debt. A sympathetic and careful student of African history, Hardy was among the first Europeans who attempted to view African history as a separate unit of study.

Towards 1884 the most favored European nations only possessed the embryos of colonies in Africa: trading posts slowly transformed into territorial domains, ports of call, and poorly delineated spheres of influence. It can be stated that the real conquest of Africa began by way of the temperate regions or by what might be called, without exaggeration, White Africa.

This first partition constituted a revolution in international politics and a great change in the history of Africa. Two states, France and England, had taken the lion's share. By contrast those states which had in past centuries played the most active roles in North Africa had either been entirely ejected from the area, as in the instance of Portugal; or had been admitted there only as poor relatives, as in the case of Italy and especially Spain—which possessed nothing more than some isolated spots on the Moroccan coast. It is true that these poor relatives could hope to retaliate in two countries which had up to this point preserved their independence, Morocco and Tripoli; but it was impossible to begin their occupation without raising serious conflicts.

Thus divided among the powerful European states, the countries of temperate Africa offered, in addition to their inherent value, another interest: they constituted bases of operations; they became the beginnings of the great European empires in Africa. In short, it

From Georges Hardy, *Vue générale de l'histoire d'Afrique*, 2nd ed. (Paris: Librairie Armand Colin, 1930), pp. 124–137. Used by permission of Librairie Armand Colin and the author. Translated by Irene and Raymond Betts.

was from White Africa that Europe was to launch its attack on Black Africa.

Hereafter, Europe was enticed into this latter region by a very obvious development of public opinion. The partition of temperate Africa had been the work of governments more than of nations; but public opinion had been enchanted by the discovery of those countries so close to Europe and as rich in natural resources as in beauty. In the eyes of contemporaries the African mirage replaced the old American mirage. The exploratory movement was thus strengthened, and acquired a new direction, a more practical one. African imperialism was born.

At the same time that it stimulated the desire for territorial possessions, the occupation of temperate Africa allowed the European peoples to learn the difficult profession of colonizer. One can be certain that the whole of French Africa, for instance, would be quite inferior to what it is in quality and in quantity if the majority of those who worked to create it had not had the opportunity of acquiring a serious colonial education in Algeria.

Compelled along this new and inviting way, Europe was soon to see its international relations become more and more complicated. The political arena was suddenly extended and the conditions of competition transformed. Instead of fighting, as in the eighteenth century, in the colonies for Europe, the Europeans were at that moment on the point of fighting in Europe for the colonies, this development occurring because the colonies tended to be incorporated into the nation and ceased to be simple pawns.

. . . Preoccupied by grave continental problems and then by the conquest of Africa until about 1884, Europe hardly dreamed of colonizing Black Africa. She continued to consider it as a world apart, greater in deceptions than in real profits.

The states which did not yet have colonial domains were not anxious to establish themselves there. Germany, in particular, affirmed its resolution to be a continental European empire. The Portuguese allowed their possessions to waste away. Spain remained obsessed by the desire to reestablish itself in Morocco. Italy was occupied in Tunisia and Abyssinia. And England lent only feeble attention to its trading posts on the Gulf of Guinea. France alone, since 1817, rather feverishly imposed on the Senegal vast "plans of colonization." Faidherbe, adding his genius to the experience of his predecessors, pacified, organized, enriched the country, and transformed it into a veritable colony. He made it the gateway to the Sudan and, moreover, prepared the way for French installation on the coast of the Gulf of Guinea.

But new occurrences put an end to this exceptional situation. Toward 1884 Black Africa became the theater and the prey of intense competition.

This development was the result of the different series of events that we have surveyed: the explorations which concluded with the European discovery of the real resources of Equatorial and tropical Africa, as well as the discovery of its social and political misery; the occupation of temperate Africa which invited extension. Above all, the economy of the civilized world had been noticeably altered since the middle of the century. All values had been transformed by the application of steam and electricity; everywhere the factory tended to replace the shop and certain peoples of recent national organization —like Germany and the United States—rivalled the old industrial nations in their traditional markets. From these developments arose the desire to find both substantial markets and abundant reservoirs of raw materials in the newly discovered regions.

Thus the European states found themselves involved in the colonization of Black Africa. Even those who rebelled at the idea were forced to yield to it, most notably Germany.

Thanks to its unification and to the financial activity which the French indemnity of five million francs had engendered, Germany had suddenly revealed, immediately after the War of 1870–1871, astonishing economic aptitudes, and Bismarck, with his exceptionally clear view of the interests of his country, adapted his theories to these new conditions thus causing a total political change. In 1884 he declared loud and clear that Germany intended to become a colonial power and that despite the late hour she wished to have her part of Africa. Although he encountered vigorous opposition in Germany, and neighboring states—except, perhaps, England—pretended not to take seriously this growling of the old bull dog, as usual, Bismarck accompanied his proposals with significant acts.

The great explorer Nachtigal was chosen as the instrument of this policy. In that same year of 1884, on the pretext of examining on the spot complaints made by German traders, he visited the west coast of Africa aboard a warship and planted the German flag on unoccupied territory. In a few months, the Togo, the Cameroons, and South-West Africa were proclaimed colonies of the German Empire, and the chancellor simply contented himself with notifying the powers of this *fait accompli.*

On the east coast, Karl Peters, who had founded in Berlin the "Society for Colonization," signed numerous treaties with native princes and entrusted the economic exploitation of the regions explored by him to the *Deutsche Ost-Afrikanische Gesellschaft* [German East African Society], a charter company protected by the Emperor of Germany. Henceforth the Germans could menace the valley of the Nile at its sources.

This rapid series of acquisitions had the effect of a sharp blow on the European states. Suddenly Black Africa acquired in their eyes its true interest. Once again Germany was, in the words of Bismarck, the bait which set the other fish stirring. . . . What occurred was a scramble, or, as it has been called, a rush. Each people disclosed rights acquired in the most disinherited regions as well as in the richest. They hastened to sign treaties with native princes more or less qualified to pawn the independence and the interests of their tribesmen. They also intervened in the quarrels of succession, always easy to find or to provoke. The result was a pillage which was given the appearance of regular negotiation, indeed of an inheritance.

Exploration took on a decided political character and suddenly became what it promised to be for some time: an affair of state. At the same time, the large groups which had dedicated themselves to the scientific discovery of Africa and the betterment of native races leaned in the direction of these selfish interests. In particular, the International African Association, founded in 1876 under the honorary presidency of the King of the Belgians and the actual presidency of Ferdinand de Lesseps and Cardinal Lavigerie, primate of Africa, was not slow in being enlisted into the imperialism of Leopold II. It was under these auspices that Stanley, a hired explorer, retook the road to Africa and prepared the organization of the Congo Free State.

The rivals sought to block the way of one another so that this partition of Black Africa appeared rich in conflict from its beginning.

But at the same time that it provoked the crisis, Germany took the initiative in obtaining its remedy.

On the occasion of a legal dispute which brought the King of the Belgians, Portugal and England into conflict, the German government invited the European powers and the United States to be represented at the "Conference" of Berlin and proposed to them the elaboration of a sort of international code which would permit the regulation of the partition of Black Africa and give it an official status.

In effect the Berlin Conference established the following principles:

1. Navigation would be free on the Niger and the Congo even in time of war;

2. The basin of the Congo would be placed under the system of free trade;

3. Every acquisition of territory on the coasts of the African continent would have to be reported without delay to the signatory powers in order to let them indicate their claims, should there be any;

4. No annexations would be valid if the sovereign state did not maintain in the territories that it claimed to occupy sufficient authority to assure the respect of the rights acquired by other states, if this was the case, and to assure freedom of trade;

5. Every European power established on the coast acquired as a result of this fact the rights to the hinterlands and could extend the limits of its possessions until it encountered a neighboring sphere of influence or an organized state.

Five years later the Conference of Brussels expanded this African code. While the Berlin Conference was exclusively concerned with the rights of the conquerors, the Brussels conference applied itself especially to the rights of the native populations. It studied the means of combatting the slave trade, the importation of fire arms, traffic in alcohol, and porterage.

The conquests, after being regulated, were humanized.

. . . Outside of their regular sessions at Berlin the powers came to an understanding about the partition of Central Africa. The Congo Free State, the domain of the International Association, was officially recognized, its boundaries traced; its neutrality reserved for it a useful role as a buffer state in those regions keenly desired. France kept the basin of the Kwilu-Niari, that is, the route of access to Brazzaville;

the German protectorate over the Cameroons continued; and Portugal retained only the two cities of Landana and Cabinda on the right bank of the Congo.

Afterwards, the obligation imposed on the powers to give notice of their acquisitions of conquests led them to collate their rights, to instigate arbitrations, and, in the final analysis, to conclude agreements for the determination of their spheres of influence. From this resulted a long series of treaties of partition, of which the history, mixed with all the debates on European politics, is very complicated, but which can be grouped according to large regions.

In eastern Africa, it was England which provided the greatest effort, but she encountered numerous rivals. She came to agreement with little difficulty with Italy over the establishment of the common boundaries of the Egyptian Sudan and Ethiopia (1891), then of the coast of Aden and of Harar (1894). On the other hand she was at first obliged to make large concessions to Germany on the coast of Zanzibar (1887), which she easily succeeded in reducing in 1890, following revolts provoked by German brutality. Above all, she found herself at odds with France at the moment when she obtained from the Congo Free State the cession of a strip of territory which enabled her to connect her positions, official or not, from the north to the south of Africa and to bar France from the route to the upper Nile. Faced with the protests of France, the Congo Free State retracted, and France and England quickly struggled for the occupation of the upper Nile. It was England which succeeded, at Fashoda (1898), with the French government, bowing before the *fait accompli,* admitting as the boundary of its sphere of influence, the line of division of the waters between the tributaries of the Nile and the Congo.

In South Africa, the region situated between the coastal colonies, the Orange River, and the Congo State was coveted simultaneously by the Boers of the Transvaal, the Portuguese, the Germans and the English. By piecemeal annexation Germany was rapidly approaching the Boer republics. However, since 1885, England, through the establishment of its protectorate over Bechuanaland, pushed a spearhead between the Germans and the Boers and imposed, by intimidation, clearly defined limits on the German possessions. Against the Boers and the Portuguese it was the famous chartered company directed by Cecil Rhodes which led the struggle. Both were stopped in their expansion, and English South Africa bordered the Congo Free State.

At Madagascar, French influence, established since the seventeenth century, was breeched by the commercial activities and political and religious intrigues of the English. The French protectorate over Madagascar had been recognized by treaties in good and due form (1885 and 1890), but the role of the residents was endlessly thwarted by the bad faith and warlike tastes of the Hovas, secretly associated with English missionaries. In 1895, after a last attempt at conciliation, France decided to end this resistance by force and then renewed the treaty of protectorate. In 1896 the protectorate was changed into direct annexation.

In West Africa, the struggle was particularly centered around the Niger and between England and France. Around 1885 France possessed the upper waters and England the mouth of the river. Where would the ultimate domain of the one and the other stop? Following some harsh campaigns, France, in 1890, acquired some important advantages: she was mistress of the river up to Timbuctu; the protectorate of Futa-Jalon joined her possessions from the coast of Guinea to Senegalese and Nigerian territories; and the coast of Dahomey provided a base for expansion towards the lower Niger. It was then that the Royal Niger Company, established in the lower regions of the Niger and the Benue, sent up a cry of alarm: it insisted that its rights were imperiled by French expansion. Its claims led to the agreement of August 5, 1890, by virtue of which the French and English spheres of influence were separated by a line passing from Say on the Niger to Barrua on the Tchad.

This time the English had gotten the better part, the most developed and fertile lands; but France made the best of its advantages. Despite constant English opposition, she achieved the conquest of the territory at the bend of the Niger, checked the expansion of the Gold Coast and Togo toward the north of Sierra Leone, effectively took possession of Dahomey, destroyed the empire of Rabah and seized that of Bornu. Then she established a solid liaison by way of the Tchad between the territories of Algeria, West Africa and Equatorial Africa. By the agreement of June 14, 1898, England recognized the result of these efforts.

In sum, by the end of the nineteenth century, this great whirlwind

which had so closely mixed the destinies of Africa and Europe sub-
sided and allowed equilibrium. In a willy-nilly fashion, the European
rivals had ended by assuming a fixed place in the various regions of
Africa, and a whole collection of treaties seemed to guarantee the
stability of the partition.

However, two great causes of imbalance existed beneath the
surface: the spirit of independence among certain indigenous societies and the poorly satisfied imperialism of some European nations.

. . . Europe disposed of Africa truly as if Africa had been an
empty land—*res nullius.* But in general African societies did not seem
willing to renounce so readily their independence. This partition of
Africa was thus quite theoretical; there still remained the question of
realizing it, that is, of making the local populations accept it.

Nearly everywhere effective occupation was difficult. War occurred in often terrifying form: mountain war, jungle war, swamp
war, desert war, etc. Europe, as well armed and valiant as she was,
did not always have the upper hand, and it was sometimes necessary
to abandon an area after great sacrifice.

Moreover, in the strict sense of the word, conquest has always
been but one step in occupation; as a general rule, it has been necessary to complete occupation by means of pacification. Even today,
certain long claimed regions are scarcely subdued and the European
presence there is only accepted on the condition of limitation or
even postponement of European demands.

These resistances have varied origins and appeals.

In all of the regions penetrated or simply lightly touched by Islam,
there are religious uprisings, of a sort comparable to the uprising of
Abd-el-Kadir in Algeria; to the insurrection of the Kabylie, then of
South Oran during the Second Empire; to the general uprising in
Algeria following upon the War of 1870 and the Cremieux Decrees
which granted French citizenship to Jews. Moreover, there are the
instances of insurrection of southern Tunisia following the establishment of the French protectorate; the revolt of the Mahdists or Der-
vishes in the Egyptian Sudan—a revolt which lasted more than ten
years, was very costly to England, but which served as a pretext for
her continued occupation of Egypt; the rebellion in German East
Africa; the opposition of the empire of El Hadj Omar to French
conquests; and so forth.

El Hadj Omar, despite his brutality, retained the appearance of a prophet, but Samory was nothing more than a bandit of some intelligence, and his case was not an isolated one. Numerous were those adventurers who, in the disorder of Africa, struck out against the foreigner with no other purpose than personal ambition. For example, Rabah, whom the French encountered in their advance toward the Tchad, was only a religious leader. Less interesting still, were the slave traders of Arab origin who, in East Africa up to the Congo, aroused the hatred of the European by continuing to tyrannize without restraint the native populations and appearing from time to time, like the famous Tippu-Tib, so formidable that it was necessary to compromise with them.

In certain regions of Africa the reigning dynasties maintained a real authority and it was from them that resistance came, notably in Madagascar and Dahomey.

Elsewhere it was simply the spirit of ethnic independence which led to opposition against European establishment, the more vigorously so as the population was savage and the region difficult to penetrate. Some, especially the Nomads, resisted the protection of the civilized, because it would impede their habits of plundering and disturb their conditions of existence. Others, like the Herero in German South-West Africa, knew from experience that the intentions of the Europeans were not always benevolent and preferred a merciless struggle to mass enslavement. Lastly, there were others who, being totally ignorant of the Europeans, feared everything from them, and, especially in the forest regions, yielded their land only foot by foot.

It is necessary to separate from this list of resistances the national uprisings which were most limited in number. Two were, so to speak, traditional and are found recurring at different moments in African history.

In Egypt the opposition was as much of a national character as religious. Religion was here only the pretext, the standard of revolt, and Egypt did not count upon either Islam or the intervention of the Christians to prove its nationalism.

In Abyssinia, the Ras of Tigre, beaten by the Italians, came to an understanding with Menelik and recognized his superiority. With the unity of the country reestablished, Menelik directly notified all the powers of his succession to the throne. Italy vainly protested and then decided upon war. She quickly overcame the troops of Tigre, but Menelik called together all the Ethiopian chiefs and addressed them in this language: "An enemy has crossed the seas and invaded our frontiers for the purpose of destroying our land and our religion. . . . With the aid of God, I will defend the heritage of our ancestors and I will repel the invader by means of arms. Those who have the strength, support me; those who have not, pray for us!" This became, as can be seen, a national movement: 150,000 men answered the call to arms, and the Italian army was roundly defeated in 1896. The complete independence of Ethiopia was recognized, while the Italian colonial dream once again vanished.

The national uprising of the Boers was of an entirely different character. It can hardly be explained by the presence and influence of a national design. It was the act of a people of relatively recent national formation, but a people who imported from Europe the concept of nationhood.

Although their independence had been recognized, the two republics of the Orange and the Transvaal were underhandedly threatened. They were reduced to the condition of enclaves; all development was forbidden to them; and the least incident might have caused them to fall into the hands of the English. This incident was the discovery of diamond mines in the Republic of Transvaal and of gold veins in the Transvaal. The entire economy of southern Africa was sharply altered. Thousands of adventurers from all nations flooded into the country, and the Boers, whose peaceful and simple existence was disturbed by this invasion, attempted to stem the flood of foreigners, or "Uitlanders." They obstinately refused the foreigners naturalization and, consequently, the right to vote; they levied enormous duties on the products necessary for the exploitation of the mines, etc. In 1895 the Uitlanders resolved to overthrow President Kruger whom they considered their principal adversary, and placed their cause in the hands of Cecil Rhodes. Simultaneously, the Boers were represented to English public opinion as ruthless slave owners; and at the right moment a humanitarian movement, "philokaffir," reinforced the economic and political interests.

The conspiracy was exposed and Europe was disturbed; but difficulties continued to become aggravated between England and the two republics. Finally, in 1899, war broke out. It was, as is known, brutal. Improvised militiamen, the Boers were indefatigable horsemen and excellent marksmen. They knew expertly how to take advantage of the difficult terrain, and they were above all moved by a holy rage. They inflicted serious setbacks on the English, but the numbers and abundance of English material resources caused their defeat. In 1902 the exhausted Boers renounced their independence, in return for which the English promised to soon grant them their autonomy and to reconstruct their devastated country.

In conclusion one sees that the resistances taking place in Africa, whatever their origins and tendencies, provoked the European states to wars of conquest and generally precipitated the occupation of the hinterlands, and thus completed the construction of the great colonial empires.

Roland Oliver and J. D. Fage

THE NEWNESS OF THE SCRAMBLE AND PROBLEMS IN ITS REALIZATION

Roland Oliver and J. D. Fage were already old Africanists while still rather young men. Oliver is a professor in the University of London, while Fage is director of the Center of West African Studies in the University of Birmingham. Both men are also editors of the highly respected Journal of African History. *No single study of African history has yet replaced their* Short History of Africa *which first appeared in 1962 and which is often used as a basic text in courses on African history.*

In 1879, despite the steady increase in the power of the western European nations compared with that of other peoples in the world, only a small proportion of the African continent was under European rule. Algeria was French, but elsewhere in North Africa it was only in Egypt and in Tunis that there existed even the beginnings of European control. In West Africa, where Europeans had had commercial dealings with the coastal peoples for four centuries, it was only in

From Roland Oliver and J. D. Fage, *A Short History of Africa* (Harmondsworth, England, 1962), pp. 181–195. Reprinted by permission of Penguin Books Ltd.

French Senegal and on the British Gold Coast that there were colonial administrations ruling any considerable number of Africans. Only in the Senegal had European rule penetrated more than a few dozen miles inland. The British colonies of the Gambia, Sierra Leone, and Lagos were no more than small enclaves in a political world still dominated by African governments. In the region which was to become Portuguese Guinea, there was Portuguese influence but hardly Portuguese rule. South of the Bight of Benin, the French colony on the Gaboon consisted of little more than the small naval station and freed-slave community of Libreville. Apart from five or six coastal towns, Portuguese Angola and Moçambique were hardly colonies in the modern sense, but rather ill-defined trading preserves reaching towards the interior.

North of Moçambique, even the coast was still virtually untouched by European political power. British diplomatic influence was strong in Zanzibar. The French had occupied the Comoros and also had a foothold in Madagascar. On the mainland, however, it was only in the extreme northeast that any European flag had yet been planted. This was a consequence of the Suez Canal, the construction of which had led France to seek a counterpoise to the British coaling station at Aden by establishing a base on the inhospitable Somali coast at Obok. The only really deep penetration of Africa by European governments was in the extreme south, but here the position was complicated by the hostility between the British colonies on the coast and the Afrikaner communities in the interior.

Two decades later, however, at the beginning of the twentieth century, European governments were claiming sovereignty over all but six of some forty political units into which they had by then divided the continent—and of these six exceptions, four were more technical than real. This partition of Africa at the end of the nineteenth century was by no means a necessary consequence of the opening up of Africa by Europeans during the first three-quarters of the century. Very few indeed of the explorers of Africa had been sent by their governments to spy out the land for later conquest. It is probably safe to say that not a single missionary had ever imagined himself as serving in the vanguard of colonialism. In so far as there was an economic motive for partition of the kind suggested by Marxist writers, it was a motive which appealed to those European powers which had no colonies and little commercial influence in Africa, rather than to those whose influence was already established there. The partition of Africa was indeed essentially the result of the appearance on the African scene of one or two powers which had not previously shown any interest in the continent. It was this that upset the preexisting balance of power and influence and precipitated a state of international hysteria in which all the powers rushed in to stake claims to political sovereignty and to bargain furiously with each other for recognition in this or that region.

The first of these new factors to enter the African scene was not strictly speaking a power. It was a European sovereign acting in his personal capacity, though using his status as a sovereign to manipulate the threads of international diplomacy in pursuit of his private objective. King Leopold II of the Belgians was a man whose ambitions and capacities far outran the introverted preoccupations of the country he had been born to rule. His interest in founding an overseas empire had started in the 1850s and 1860s when as Duke of Brabant he had travelled in Egypt and had also scanned possible openings in places as remote as Formosa, Sarawak, Fiji, and the New Hebrides. Succeeding to the throne in 1865, he bent most of his great energies to the study of African exploration. Ten years later he was ready to act. His cover was the African International Association, created in 1876 to found a chain of commercial and scientific stations running across central Africa from Zanzibar to the Atlantic. The stations were to be garrisoned, and they were to serve as bases from which to attack the slave trade and to protect Christian missions. The first two expeditions of the association entered East Africa from Zanzibar in 1878 and 1879, and attached themselves to mission stations of the White Fathers at Tabora and on Lake Tanganyika. From this moment, however, Leopold's interests switched increasingly to the west coast of Bantu Africa. Stanley, who in 1877 had completed his coast-to-coast journey by descending the Congo River, took service under King Leopold in 1879, and during the next five years established a practicable land and water transport system from the head of the Congo estuary to Stanley Falls, more than a thousand miles upstream, at the modern Stanleyville.

Leopold, meanwhile, was deftly preparing the way for international recognition of his rule over the whole area of the Congo basin. Al-

FIGURE 4. A portrait by Jef Leempoels of Leopold II, King of the Belgians, as he appeared in old age. Source: Frontispiece from Henry W. Wach, *The Story of the Congo* (New York: G. P. Putnam's, 1905).

though his real intention was to develop his colony on the basis of a close-fisted commercial monopoly, he was successful in persuading a majority of the European powers that it would be preferable to have the Congo basin as a free-trade area under his "international" regime than to let it fall to any of their national rivals. The skill of King Leopold's diplomacy has been widely recognized. What has received less notice is the extent to which it sharpened the mutual suspicions of the European powers about their activities in Africa as a whole. Probably it was Leopold, more than any other single statesman, who created the "atmosphere" of scramble.

The next power to enter the African scene was Germany. Acting with stealth and swiftness in the eighteen months from the end of 1883 to the beginning of 1885, Germany made extensive annexations in four widely-separated parts of the continent—South-West Africa, Togoland, the Cameroons, and East Africa. It was this German action which was really to let loose the scramble on a scale bound to continue with ever-increasing intensity until the whole continent was partitioned. It is therefore the more remarkable that recent historical research has tended to show that Germany entered Africa, not primarily in order to satisfy a desire for empire there, but rather as part of a much wider design to deflect French hostility against her in Europe by fomenting rivalries in Africa and by creating a situation in which Germany would be the arbiter between French and British ambitions.

The key to this situation lay in Egypt. Here in 1881 the joint Anglo-French financial control had broken down in face of the revolt of the national army, led by one of its most senior Egyptian officers, Arabi Pasha, with the tacit sympathy of the puppet Khedive Taufiq. France and Britain planned to act in concert to destroy Arabi, but on the eve of the operation a domestic crisis prevented the French government from participating. In consequence, the British invaded Egypt alone in 1882, and remained there, despite promises of withdrawal, as the *de facto* though not *de jure* rulers of the country until the declaration of a British protectorate in 1914. The continued British occupation of Egypt angered the French and encouraged them to develop their formal empire in West Africa. This suited Germany, and it also gave Germany the means of twisting the British arm without openly supporting France, for British rule in Egypt was only possible with the support of a majority of Egypt's creditors represented on the international Caisse de la Dette, and this majority was controlled by Germany. Throughout the vital years of partition Germany supported British rule in Egypt, but at the price of British acquiescence in German actions throughout the rest of the continent. The German annexations were intended to incite the French to further action in Africa, but to action directed more against Britain than against Germany. In this way the painful subject of Alsace and Lorraine would be forgotten in the Anglo-French rivalry over Africa.

Such then was the motivation for the scramble. To the three powers already engaged on the African coastline—Britain, France, and Portugal—there were now added two more, one of them a European sovereign in search of a personal empire, the other the strongest state in continental Europe, seeking to induce the most recent victim of its aggression to wear out its resentment in colonial adventure. In the circumstances, partition was bound to follow. Of the five powers mainly concerned, only King Leopold was positively anxious for a widespread territorial empire. Of the others, however, none was prepared to stand aside and see the continent swallowed by its rivals. And it was only a matter of time before Italy and Spain would likewise each claim a share. Deeply as it was to affect all the peoples of the continent, the partition was in its origin essentially a projection into Africa of the international politics of Europe. The new map of Africa which emerged from partition bore little relation to the activities of Europeans in Africa during its earlier periods.

As it happened, the first to secure international recognition of a large African empire was King Leopold. In 1884, after the British merchants engaged in the Congo trade had opposed their government's intention of recognizing Portuguese claims to the lower Congo region, Portugal changed tack and instead appealed to France and Germany for support. France, seeing a chance to embarrass Britain, agreed to Bismarck's suggestion of determining the Congo question by an international conference in Berlin. And even before this conference could meet, France (having made a deal with King Leopold by which she secured the reversion of his Congo empire in case its development became too much for his resources) had joined Germany and the United States in granting recognition to the "Congo Free State." When the conference met in December 1884, the other powers had no option but to follow suit.

The Berlin Conference passed many high-sounding resolutions on the slave trade, on free trade, and on the need to prove effective occupation before fresh annexations were declared. In fact, however, the six months during which the conference was being prepared had seen the most flimsily-supported annexations in the whole partition, those of Germany herself. While the conference was actually sitting,

Bismarck announced his government's protectorate over those parts of East Africa where Karl Peters and his associates had obtained dubious treaties from bemused and often bogus "chiefs" in the course of a single expedition lasting a few weeks. It was now clear to all that a quick partition of the whole continent was inevitable, and the delegates went home from Berlin at the beginning of 1885 to consider where further claims for their own countries could most usefully be developed.

The logic of earlier interests made it inevitable that the French African empire should expand first within the western bulge of the continent. By 1883 their war against Ahmadu, which they had begun in 1879, had brought the French to the upper Niger. It was natural that they should think first of expanding along the internal line of communications offered by this great river, and then of connecting their conquests with their spheres of influence on the coast. But their advance down the Niger was slow; Timbuctu was not reached until 1893. One reason for this was that the French right flank lay in Mande country, where there had arisen a national and Islamic hero, Samori, fully determined to maintain his people's historic tradition of independence. Samori was not finally overcome until 1898, and it was not till some two years before this that the French were able to resume their westward advance.

During the 1880s, the future of the French Gaboon remained less certain. Although King Leopold's activities on the lower Congo had stimulated the French to develop a treaty network in the area explored by de Brazza, it was not until the nineties that they began to drive expeditions northwards to meet the expanding frontiers of French West Africa at Lake Chad, and northeastwards up the Ubangui to threaten the upper Nile.

For Britain the strategy of expansion was by no means so obvious as for France. Southern Africa was one possible growing-point. It was also, however, a region where Britain had already been compelled to recognize the independence of the Boer republics, and where it was now faced with extensive German annexations on the southwestern side of the peninsula. Northward expansion from the Cape had therefore to take place through the bottleneck of Bechuanaland, hastily annexed in 1885 to counter the Germans. Moreover, although the British government had to handle the diplomacy of partition and to acquire the nominal sovereignty, this was a region where the practical initiative necessarily lay with the Europeans of the Cape Colony. Among these the most active figure was Cecil Rhodes, a British settler who had made a vast fortune out of the amalgamation of the diamond mines at Kimberley in Griqualand West. In response to his pressure, the British government in 1888 declared the existence of a British sphere of interest between Bechuanaland and the Zambezi. In 1889, by Royal Charter, it delegated the functions of government in this region to Rhodes's British South Africa Company.

In Africa north of the Zambezi, wider options had to be exercised. Commercially the most valuable region lay in West Africa, and there were many who thought that other interests should be sacrificed for the sake of an advantageous partition of this part of Africa between Britain and France. It is in fact probable that at any time during the eighties there would have been terms on which the French would have left the British an unbroken sphere from Sierra Leone to the Cameroons; and a British withdrawal from East Africa could probably also have produced a German withdrawal from the west coast. The first of any such terms, however, would have been a British withdrawal from Egypt, and this was a thing which no British government after 1885 would even contemplate. Indeed, Lord Salisbury, who as prime minister and foreign secretary handled the British side of partition during the decisive years from 1886 to 1892, built the whole of his African policy around the retention of Egypt. This meant in the first place a deliberate encouragement of French expansion in the west, to the point of doing nothing to prevent the encirclement of the four well-established British spheres along the coast. It meant, therefore, looking for the main British share in the partition on the eastern side of the continent, even though it was commercially almost valueless, and even though it must in the long run prove expensive to occupy. The Germans were already entrenched on the mainland opposite Zanzibar, but in 1886 Salisbury was able to demarcate the rough limits of a British sphere of influence in what is now Kenya, while holding open the possibility of a British Uganda and of a "back door" to the Sudan and Egypt. In East Africa, as in Zambezia and in central and northern Nigeria, a Chartered Company's willingness to take the responsibility for administration lay at the back of Salisbury's decision to negotiate at the international level.

There remained only the additional claims to what is now Northern Rhodesia and Nyasaland, formulated in 1889–1890, and Salisbury's design was complete. In 1890 and 1891 he proceeded to delimitation with Germany, France, Portugal, and Italy. The most important of these agreements was that with Germany. Though often described as the exchange of Heligoland for Zanzibar, Britain in fact ceded Heligoland to Germany as part of a settlement which defined most of the new Anglo-German frontiers in Africa in a manner satisfactory to Salisbury. The agreement with Italy fixed the frontier between the British East African protectorate and the newly-claimed Italian colony in Somalia. The two Anglo-Portuguese agreements of 1890 and 1891, though imposed in a high-handed way by a strong power upon a weaker one, definitively settled the frontiers between British Central Africa and its Portuguese neighbors. It was the Anglo-French agreement which was the least satisfactory of the four, since it left the inland frontiers in West Africa undecided, and since it failed to touch upon the all-important question of the Sudan.

The most remarkable aspect of the first ten years of the scramble for Africa was the extent to which almost everything of importance happened in Europe. Statesmen and diplomats met in offices or country houses and drew lines across maps which themselves were usually inaccurate. Often the lack of geographical detail was such that frontiers had to be traced along lines of latitude and longitude. In Africa itself the reality of partition was slight indeed. A dozen over-worked men could make up the local representatives of a Chartered Company. A consul and two assistants might well form the government of a protectorate. Such establishments were apt to be too busy keeping themselves alive to engage in military collisions with neighboring governments. Even if rival teams were racing for a treaty in the same area, it was most unlikely that their paths would cross. The conflicting claims would be sorted out a year later round a table in some European capital.

As the scramble passed into its second decade, however, the activities of the men on the spot assumed a new significance. The position of interior frontiers often depended upon which of two neighboring powers was able to create something like effective occupation. Encounters between the nationals of different European powers became increasingly frequent. They happened especially along the western frontiers of Nigeria, where (after the French had conquered the native kingdom of Dahomey in 1893) fairly substantial military forces threatened to collide in the disputed territory of Borgu. The hurry to reach Borgu before the French also involved Goldie's Royal Niger Company in its first military clashes with the African states lying within its chartered sphere. To forestall the French in Borgu, it was necessary to conquer the emirates of Nupe and Ilorin.

Again, by the later nineties French expeditions were converging on Lake Chad from three directions, from the French Congo, from Algeria, and from the upper Niger, and for a brief time the dream of a vast French empire linking the Mediterranean, the Atlantic, and the Indian Ocean caught the imagination of the French public. A French occupation of the upper Nile would strike a vital blow at the British in Egypt. From 1896 until 1898, therefore, Commandant Marchand pushed a painful passage with a small company of native soldiers all the way from the Gaboon to Fashoda on the White Nile, some four hundred miles south of Khartoum. Britain in 1885 had compelled Egypt to abandon its former dominion in the Nilotic Sudan to the forces of the Mahdi, Muhammed Ahmad, on the grounds that Egypt could not then afford the expense of reconquest. Salisbury, however, had never lost sight of the Sudan; in 1896, after a disastrous defeat inflicted upon the Italians by the French-armed troops of Menelik of Abyssinia, the new Egyptian army trained by Kitchener was ordered to begin the southward advance. The province of Dongola fell the same year, Berber in 1897, Khartoum itself after the battle of Omdurman in September 1898. A week later Kitchener heard of Marchand's presence at Fashoda, and hastened to confront him with a vastly superior force: the "Fashoda incident" brought France and Britain to the brink of war. This well-known fact of history has tended to obscure another, which is that Kitchener's reconquest of the Sudan, at a conservative estimate, cost the death in battle of twenty thousand Sudanese. The partition of Africa, as it approached its logical conclusion, was beginning to be a bloody business.

The crowning bloodshed, however, was that inflicted by white men on white in South Africa. Here the discovery of the vast gold wealth of the Witwatersrand in 1886 had given enormous potential power to the Transvaal, hitherto the poorest and weakest of the European communities. And this was clearly appreciated by both the titans of the South African scene—by Paul Kruger, president of the Transvaal from 1883 to 1902, and by Cecil Rhodes, who had extended his mining interests from Kimberley to the Witwatersrand and who, from 1890 to 1896, was also prime minister of the Cape Colony. To Kruger's ambition of creating a united white South Africa under Boer republican leadership, Rhodes opposed a larger dream. He envisaged a federation of South Africa, where Boer, Briton, and even conceivably the Bantu might achieve the closest harmony. Such a federation would be internally self-governing but would maintain a strong connection with Britain and the British Empire, the extension of which Rhodes once described as his only religion. Kruger, then, represented a seventeenth-century Afrikaner ethos making belated attempts to adapt itself to new circumstances; Rhodes was the local embodiment of the new capitalist imperialism of the late nineteenth and early twentieth centuries, which in South Africa had a predominantly British coloring.

In the opening stages of the conflict, as we have seen, Rhodes had concentrated on turning the Transvaal flank; he had helped to maneuver the British government into Bechuanaland, and had obtained a Royal Charter to govern the region to the north of it. In 1890 he sent his pioneer column of policemen and settlers to occupy the Mashona territories to the east and northeast of Matabeleland. In 1891 the operational sphere of his company was extended to include most of what is now Northern Rhodesia. Rhodes believed that these measures, as well as being the first steps in the northward expansion he sought for British rule, would encircle the Transvaal and so drive it into closer cooperation with the Cape Colony. He hoped that the minerals of the new territories in the north would enable the Cape to match the wealth of the Transvaal. But before the new settler colony of Rhodesia could begin to take root, Rhodes's men had first to engage in unofficial war with the Portuguese from Moçambique, then to conquer a Matabele nation bitterly resentful of their presence, and finally to overcome a rising of both Matabele and Mashona occasioned by the settlers' demands for land and labor. Fighting did not cease until 1897. Even then, the promised gold of the Monomatapas' former empire proved disappointing, and also (until the coming of the railways from the Cape and from Beira in 1899) very costly to extract.

In relation to the Transvaal, all Rhodes had succeeded in doing was to convince Kruger that the very existence of his country was at stake, and to determine him to cut loose from the rest of South Africa by securing the completion of the Transvaal's own railway to the Portuguese port at Delagoa Bay. He was thus able to keep out of the customs union and the integrated railway system from the ports in the Cape and Natal, with which Rhodes had been hoping to enmesh him. Meanwhile, the integrity of Kruger's Boer republic was being menaced from within by the growing numbers and wealth of the *Uitlanders,* the foreigners drawn to the Transvaal by its mining industry. The old informal Boer ideas of government had given way before a new administrative machine, staffed by educated Nether- landers, which insisted on the *Uitlanders* subscribing to Afrikaner ideals before sharing in political rights. Rhodes, always an im- patient man, retaliated by mounting the Jameson Raid of 1896, in an attempt to replace Kruger's government by an *Uitlander* regime more amenable to his designs for South Africa.

The ignominious failure of the Jameson Raid ruined Rhodes politi- cally. He forfeited all claim to Afrikaner support, even in his own Cape Colony. Indeed, he convinced Afrikaners throughout South Africa that British South Africans, supported by Britain, were aiming at the overthrow of the republics and the ideals for which they stood. This was indeed the case, for the direction of British policy in South Africa now passed to Chamberlain, who had been privy to the raid plan, and to his nominee as British High Commissioner in South Africa, Sir Alfred Milner. Whereas Rhodes, for all his faults and mis- takes, was as much South African as British, or more, in his aims and outlook, Chamberlain and Milner cared nothing for local feelings, and Milner even more than his master was impelled by a belief that all South Africa had to be conquered and ruled until the Dutch ele- ment could be Anglicized. Milner deliberately pressed the *Uitlander* cause to the point of conflict, and war came at last in 1899. The help Kruger had hoped for from Britain's European rivals did not materialize. Only the Orange Free State stood by the side of its brother republic against the might of Britain and her empire. Inde- pendent Boer commandos continued the struggle long after the British armies had taken formal possession of the two republics, but by 1902 the majority of the Boers had had enough, and sought peace.

With the British conquest of the Boer republics, the European scramble for African colonies was virtually complete. Over large areas of the continent it was still mainly a paper transaction negotiated in the chancelleries of Europe, and it was only much later that its significance became apparent to most of the Africans concerned. Here and there, however, it had already provoked bitter resistance. For Ahmadu and Samori in the western Sudan, for Ashanti and Dahomey and Benin, for the Arab and Swahili slave traders of east and central Africa, for the Mahdists on the upper Nile and for the Matabele in Rhodesia, and not least for the Afrikaners in the extreme south, the coming of the European governments could only mean the destruction of their traditional ways of life and the imposition of new orders in which they could see no place for themselves. All these had fought to the best of their abilities, and lost.

Of the peoples of Africa who still remained independent by 1902, the Moroccan tribes were sheltered for a space by the mutual jealousies of the European powers. But in 1904 Britain and France composed their differences in the entente, and in 1911 France bought off the German interest by surrendering a large slice of her Congo territory to the German colony of Kamerun. Morocco could thus at last be partitioned by France and Spain. Only the Ethiopians had succeeded in holding back the flowing tide of European material power, forcing the Italians to limit themselves for some time to the dry and torrid coastlines of Eritrea and Somalia. In 1911, however, Italy sought her compensation in the conquest of Libya from the dying Turkish empire. Liberia also had precariously preserved her independence, from all but the European money-lenders. Elsewhere there could be no doubt that Africans were to enter the twentieth century under the firm control of one or other of the European colonial powers.

Endre Sik

THE SCRAMBLE AS A NECESSARY PHASE IN EUROPEAN CAPITALISTIC EXPLOITATION

Endre Sik is one of the oldest members of the Communist Party of Hungary and is former foreign minister of that state. In the first volume of his study of African history, he reveals the degree to which political polemic and sweeping generalization can be allowed to combine. The volume has been harshly reviewed, yet it has been excerpted in this study in order to demonstrate the manner in which African history, and notably the "scramble," are topics of current political debate.

Even before the decade of the 1870s the major European powers attempted to enlarge their colonial bases on the coast of Africa and to occupy adjacent territories. After the 1870s, and particularly in the 1880s, European capitalism, passing over to imperialism, sought the occupation of the entire continent. The conquest of Africa was spread over several dozen years. Colonial expansion unfolded in a bitter struggle between rival powers, complicated by the ardent resistance of the African peoples.

With the advent of imperialism, the major powers played a special role in world affairs. In effect, all of this politics reflected the economic struggle of the monopolistic groups of financial capital in the most highly developed countries of the world for the world market. As a result, after a century of relative calm, the struggle among capitalists avid for new profits took on extremely acute forms in Africa at the end of the 1870s and especially the 1880s.

Yet this struggle differed fundamentally from the struggle of "all against all" of the period of the slave trade. It differed with respect to participants, motives and objectives, as well as to its forms and scope. If, previously, it had been enterprising capitalists and their small groups (either private or governmentally supported) who com-

From Endre Sik, *Histoire de L'Afrique noire*, Vol. I (Budapest, 1961; translated into French by Frida Lederer), pp. 291, 292–293, 295–296, 297, 309–310. Translated by Irene and Raymond Betts.

peted, in the period here considered, it was the great monopolies of financial capital from the largest imperialistic countries, represented by powerful governments, who were opposed.

As the bourgeois countries developed, the power of the state gradually became that of finance capital, and the governments of the capitalistic states which had penetrated into Africa did not limit themselves to the role of proclaimed or secret patron, of various adventurers, merchants, companies, and so forth. Rather they became the active organizers of systematic competition undertaken for the acquisition of the largest number of colonial regions and for their monopolization, with the purpose of creating large colonial units forming, in toto, *colonial empires*. This struggle, in the course of which as many old and tried techniques were employed as new, was conducted on two fronts: the one against the African peoples, and the other among the rival imperialists. The objective of the struggle was no longer the conquest of bases or limited regions, but the possession of the greatest number of African lands and the exertion of control over the hinterlands which were, or would become, the sources of raw materials and areas for profitable investments. Such enterprise being inherent in the finance capitalism of each imperialist power, the conflict for African colonies was transferred into a competition for the partition of Africa among the strongest and most important powers, and essentially, England, France and Germany. As for the small powers which also possessed African colonies (Portugal, Spain and Belgium), these were only able to maintain their colonies because of the existence of divergent interests and conflicts among the major powers which, in turn, hindered them from coming to agreement on the spoils.

. . . With respect to the nature of the struggle and the methods and techniques used by the powers in Africa, these differed totally from those utilized by the adventurers and merchants of the sixteenth and seventeenth centuries. At that earlier time conflicts had an accidental character. In general, competition took the form of scuffles among the intruders for the seizure of some booty or the occupation of some base, or in the pursuit of plunder. These pirates—which the adventurers truly were while acting either for their own account or as official agents of the government—attacked one another in order to grab the prize. The "conflicts" were resolved on the spot solely by the forces which the adversaries disposed at the given moment and place.

In the decade of the 1880s and in the years that followed, financial capital led its struggle in an entirely different way. In the first place it had recourse to diplomatic intrigues systematically contrived in Europe in the form of discussions and secret agreements concluded by some imperialistic governments against others. These agreements were continually violated, annulled or concluded anew. The allies of yesterday became the adversaries of tomorrow and vice-versa. At the same time, the armed forces of the rivals were no longer thrown into battle in order to regulate minor conflicts or to lay hold of a ship or a port; they now constituted the decisive argument in the imperialistic struggle for the partition of African territories, an argument held in reserve during the course of diplomatic discussions, but always ready to be put into action if need be for the realization of envisaged plans.

The diplomatic contest between England, France and Germany, which lasted twenty years, was but the preparation for the partition of Africa by means of a great imperialistic war. Often events developed in such a manner that the armed forces of the greatest powers were face to face and ready to enter into conflict. Thus, for example, in 1884, the warships of England and Germany were on the verge of starting a battle for the Cameroons on the west coast of Africa. And in 1898 the French and British imperialists in effect undertook a military campaign in West Sudan (the Fashoda incident).

But the war never broke out and the partition of Africa unfolded among the imperialist powers without military action (if one does not count the minor incidents).

. . . In the majority of the African lands, the European occupants encountered armed resistance from the indigenous populations.

Among the least advanced peoples this resistance took the form of local, spontaneous actions, while among the more developed peoples defensive war was organized and led by the chief of tribes and tribal federations. Rare were those instances in which the imperialists managed to occupy the country without having to face the armed resistance of the African masses; and these occasions resulted only by means of deceit and corruption of chiefs, or by the pitting of one against the other.

. . . The results of the campaigns of occupation and the "peaceful agreements" of this period were different from those wars and "agreements" of the previous period.

During the *era of the slave trade* war against, and conquest of the African peoples by the European intruders meant extermination, loss of coastal territory and slavery . . . for the former. However, with the exception of some unimportant instances, these wars did not result in constant and regular contact between occupants and conquered tribes. In general, the Europeans did not meddle in the domestic life of the tribes.

In the period of *colonial activity developed by commercial and industrial capital* (that lasting until the decade of the 1870s), the situation completely changed. At this time, each military victory of the colonizers or each agreement that they concluded marked the beginning of their mingling with the natives in some form or other. The conditions of peace dictated by the intruders of this period generally contained obligations which caused changes in the economic and social life of the conquered tribes (for example, prohibition of slave trade), or the establishment of permanent contacts between the vanquished peoples and their occupiers (such as forced delivery of goods and forced labor, etc.).

. . . However, the wars of this period did not yet entirely regulate the relations between invaders and conquered peoples and did not establish the total control of the European powers over the economic, political or social life of the tribes and the African peoples. During this time the invaders subdued the peoples without always becoming the all-powerful masters of a complete people or territory.

The total occupation of the African territories and the enslavement of their peoples by the capitalists only occurred in the *period of imperialism,* following upon systematically organized campaigns directed according to well-established plans. The "pacific agreements" dictated to the conquered tribes, or the treaties signed by the chiefs, not only determined certain obligations for the conquered peoples but placed them completely under the economic and political power of foreign capital. . . .

Running counter to the conflict among the powers for the partition of Africa, the struggle of the African peoples against their invaders developed in each region and in each country according to local

PUNCH, OR THE LONDON CHARIVARI. November 28, 1906.

IN THE RUBBER COILS.

Scene—*The Congo " Free" State.*

FIGURE 5. A famous *Punch* cartoon protesting the economic exploitation of the Belgian Congo by Leopold II. Criticism of this sort was part of the Congo reform movement in England at the beginning of the twentieth century. Source: *Punch*, November 28, 1906, p. 389.

circumstances. The history . . . is closely linked to the history of the occupation and partition of the country (region) concerned and, in a minor way, especially in the first stage, linked to the struggles and events which unfolded in other African countries and regions.

. . . The period of the occupation and definitive partition of Africa (1885–1900) was that of the imperialistic war and campaigns of conquest which the European powers directed against the African peoples. In the history of the African peoples this epoch is that of the outbreak of their struggle for independence and of their just wars and insurrections.

The character of these wars and insurrections differed according to region.

At the beginning of the 1880s, there were few countries possessing an established and organized form of state and disposing of a regular army equipped according to modern techniques. Outside of the Boer republics, only Ethiopia and Madagascar were such states. As we have already observed, to conquer these countries the imperialists engaged in large and long wars. . . . To this end these states had mobilized all their human and material forces, and, in the inequal struggle which they had to pursue against the much stronger military might of their adversaries, these liberty-loving peoples demonstrated their great patriotism, heroism and freedom.

Nevertheless, in Black Africa there was no state so developed as that of the Boers, Ethiopians or Malgaches. For this reason the defensive struggle for liberty and independence in the majority of African countries took the form of a tribal liberation movement and insurrection.

. . . But neither the heroism of the tribes nor the ability and fidelity of their chiefs was able to check the attacks of the imperialists.

Kenneth Onwuka Dike

THE DEVELOPMENT OF EUROPEAN-WEST AFRICAN RELATIONS AND THE PARTITION OF AFRICA

Kenneth Onwuka Dike is part of a new generation of Africanists, an African writing about Nigerian history. Trained in the University of London, former vice-chancellor of the University of Ibadan and former ambassador of Biafra,

Reprinted from K. Onwuka Dike, *Trade and Politics in the Niger Delta, 1830–1885* (Oxford, 1956), pp. 4–5, 10–13, 18, 203–208, 214–215, 217–228, by permission of the Clarendon Press, Oxford, and the author.

he is now professor of African history at Harvard University. His volume,
Trade and Politics in the Niger Delta, 1830–1885, *first published in 1956, was*
widely acclaimed by reviewers.

In West African history the concentration of students on external
factors such as the suppression of the slave trade, the work of the
navy, the era of the explorers, the forts and settlements along the
coast, the policies and personalities of the various foreign and colonial
secretaries, has tended to submerge the history of the indigenous
peoples and to bestow undue prominence on the activities of the
invaders. As yet no comprehensive assessment of the African middlemen's position in the Atlantic slave trade exists; few if any studies
have displayed the real magnitude of the revolution brought about by
the prohibition of the traffic from 1807 or the full effects of abolition
on the existing native governments. As an instance, a major thread
in West African history—the character of the association of the
coastal kingdoms with the European traders—is treated, if at all, as
merely incidental to the subject; yet without knowledge of this association the position of power occupied by the African middlemen in
the period of the slave trade cannot be appreciated.

British prohibition of this trade, a movement which in West Africa
precipitated a radical change in the economic sphere—the trade was
the economic mainstay of all the coastal principalities—soon wrought
corresponding changes in the social and political planes. It is, of
course, a truism that up to a point a profound change in the economy
of any given community tends to bring about an unsettlement of and
a readjustment in the social organization. Such a change did occur
in nineteenth-century West Africa; in comparison with the three
centuries that preceded them, the fifty years between 1830 and 1885
were an epoch of change and revolution; it was essentially a period
of transition from a predominantly slave-trading economy to one
based on trade in the raw materials of the West African forest. A
cursory glance at the pattern of the early trade (1481–1807), is necessary not only for an understanding of its essential characteristics but
even more for an appreciation of the depth and intensity of the revolution which swept away the old order in the nineteenth century. . . .

. . . From 1481 to 1807 trade with the foreigner did not alter the
political contours of West Africa. During these centuries the flag did

not, in the main, follow trade. The lands of Guinea remained under native governments and the European concerned himself almost exclusively with trade. There were, of course, local modifications to this generalization and the degree of abstention from African politics differed from one trading area to another. In the area of the forts, more particularly in the Gold Coast, European settlements situated near African territories were inevitably involved in local politics. The colonizing experiments in Freetown, the Senegambia, the kingdom of Kongo and Angola and others were exceptions to the general rule. But the political subjection which accompanied nineteenth-century trade expansion was of recent origin and in many areas of West Africa less than a century old. With abolition the radical change in the economic sphere soon wrought corresponding changes in the social and political planes. The 400-year-old political systems built on the slave trade gradually declined and by the 1880s collapsed.

These revolutionary changes were due to a complex variety of factors, political, economic, strategic, and humanitarian, all world-wide in their implications and, although occurring in the main in Europe and America, having decisive effects on the commerce of West Africa. The slave trade, its abolition, and the economic, military, and humanitarian forces which contributed to its extinction, are more or less well known. The aspect of this many-sided movement most forcibly felt in contemporary West Africa was the economic. At the end of the eighteenth century a predominantly mercantile epoch was being succeeded by a predominantly industrial age. In Britain, where the industrial change was greatest, the slave trade, which had fitted perfectly into the scheme of mercantilist economics, was being rendered obsolete by the rapid technological advance in industrial production. Abolition of the slave trade was therefore only one manifestation of the major changes from the era of mercantilism to that of the industrial revolution and aggressive free trade.

The humanitarianism so widely advertised at the time was, in one sense, the reflection on the ideological plane of changes taking place in the economic sphere. This explains the "curious affinity" between the two forces that has been noted by many writers. The two aspects were complementary and any attempt to explain the one without reference to the other will lead to an over-simplification of a complex issue.

Consider one aspect of the economic change taking place in Britain at the time of the abolition. Towards the end of the eighteenth century Liverpool capital, reared on the slave trade, was being diverted to a new channel—the cotton trade with America. Inventions connected with the cotton industry followed each other in rapid succession. Industrialized Lancashire claimed the attention of the capitalists and of powerful slave interests. British shipping was to find employment in a new direction as the cotton trade began to render the British slave trade obsolete. The change-over was gradual, yet it was this mounting economic change which reduced slave interests to manageable proportions and enabled the abolitionists to attack it successfully. On the other hand, had it not been for the spirited and inspired attack of the Christian humanitarians such as Wilberforce and Clarkson, slavery and the slave trade might have lingered on—as indeed other decadent systems did linger on—long after they had outlived their usefulness.

It is necessary to emphasize again that these contemporary movements connected with the industrial change were a European not a West African phenomenon. This is particularly true of happenings on the ideological plane. The nineteenth-century West African middleman was not only ignorant of the ideological battle raging in Europe on the question of abolition, but his ideas of life, of society, and of man belonged to a world poles apart from that in which the Benthamites argued and the Clapham sect preached.

Along the coast of West Africa, particularly in those parts where the slave trade formed the basis of the economy of the communities concerned, opposition to abolition was the rule. In the Gold Coast, where European forts and settlements were situated close to the African states, local native resentment against the Act of 1807 led to serious riots. When Parliament rebuked the Committee of the Company of Merchants for failing to convince Africans that abolition was for the good of the natives, the committee retorted,

> *Can the wildest theorist expect that a mere act of the British legislature should in a moment inspire . . . natives of the vast continent of Africa and persuade them, nay more, make them practically believe and feel that it is for their interest to contribute to and even acquiesce in, the destruction of a trade . . . by which alone they have been hitherto accustomed to acquire wealth and purchase all the foreign luxuries and conveniences of life?*

On this point the attitude of the white slave-trader and the African middleman was identical, for the economic basis of both their lives was threatened. To contemporary Africans the European movement for abolition was extremely puzzling, especially as Englishmen who were foremost in the trade became overnight the most zealous in opposing it. Not only had the slave trade been the mainstay of their economics, but slave-trading kingdoms such as Lagos, Dahomey, Bonny, and many others owed their origin and greatness to the rise of the slave trade. The king of Bonny, Africa's greatest slave market, spoke for the rest when he declared to Captain Crow in 1807:

> We [i.e. the king and Council] think that this trade must go on. That also is the verdict of our Oracle and the priests. They say that your country, however great, can never stop a trade ordained by God himself.

Yet in spite of the determined opposition of slave interests the old order began gradually to yield place to the new. Economists argued that Africa had other commodities more lucrative than slaves to offer to the growing industries of England, and urged that the West African labor force, instead of being denuded to exploit the West Indies and the Americas, should be turned to agricultural production in Africa itself.

The new industrial order demanded above all markets and raw materials for the rising output of British factories. The quest for markets is reflected in Captain Cook's voyages in search of the "Terra Incognita Australis"—that mythical continent of the eastern Pacific that turned out to be another El Dorado. The same consideration turned Europe's attention to Africa, and in England the African Association, founded in 1788 and representing a galaxy of interests, sent expedition after expedition to scour the interior of the continent. These ventures, directly or indirectly, received government support. The student of West African history cannot fail to note that from the late eighteenth century to the end of the nineteenth there was a concerted movement, directed chiefly at first from Britain and later from France, Belgium, and Germany, to enter the West African interior, exploit its resources, and open new markets for European manufactures. . . .

The persistent search for "a highway into the heart of Central Africa," commonly known as "the quest for the course and termination of the river Niger," came at a time when the new industrialism was endowing Europe with the technical instruments of effective action in Africa. This quest Europe consciously and energetically pursued from 1788 to 1830. Eighteen thirty was the year of destiny. It was the year when the twin problems of geography and commerce were solved by the momentous discovery of the brothers Richard and John Lander that the Niger entered the Atlantic in the Bight of Biafra. Throughout Europe the event was hailed as one of cardinal importance.

> *Though the knowledge of interior Africa [said Dr. Martin Leaks, F.R.S., in a paper read in 1830 before the Royal Geographical Society] is the progressive acquisition of many enterprising men . . . it cannot be denied that the last great discovery has done more than any other to place the outline of African geography on a basis of certainty. When to this is added the consideration that it opens a maritime communication into the center of the continent, it may be described as the greatest geographical discovery that has been made since that of New Holland.*

This epoch-making event altered the emphasis, so far as the Niger basin and its Delta were concerned, from exploration to commerce. The river became to the trading Europeans an arm of the Atlantic Ocean, the main road to the gold and treasure, real and imaginary, of the vast interior. Significantly, this discovery coincided with the development of the steam engine, for had the steamboat not begun to displace the sailing ship, river navigation on a commercially important scale would not have been possible. From the thirties to the end of the century the Niger and its Delta became the focus of attention and witnessed the long series of scientific and commercial expeditions organized by the new school of inland (as opposed to coast) traders, a movement that was to make Nigeria a British protectorate. This region provides the best illustration of the process by which the trading activities of 500 years led in the nineteenth century to the political subjection of West Africa to Europe. The history of the Niger Delta in the years 1830–1885 is therefore the history of one of the highways of imperialism in West Africa; like the more famous Congo the Niger was considered a dazzling prize by the competing great powers— Britain, France, and Germany. . . .

. . . In the half-century following 1830 Britain established and maintained an "informal" or commercial empire over the Delta states. In strict constitutional sense this region was foreign territory until the proclamation of the protectorate and could not, *de jure,* be considered an integral part of the British empire. But British reluctance to annex the Delta formally was no evidence of her unwillingness to control the area politically. She achieved commercial supremacy over the coastal region through the medium of the African Squadron and from 1849 through the exertions of her consuls aided by the warships. Further, the unequal treaties concluded with the Delta states became her instruments of pressure and coercion in her dealings with native governments. Since these governments were strong enough to maintain the flow of trade between the hinterland and the coast, Britain tolerated and strengthened those city-states, such as Old Calabar and the Cameroons whose rulers collaborated in advancing her commercial interests. On the other hand, African rulers such as Pepple, king of Bonny, who refused to bend, were broken. In other words, so long as the existing native governments served her trade interests well Britain preferred the cheap informal dependency of the Delta type to the expensive formal colonies of the Gold Coast and Sierra Leone.

It has been shown that an important factor in the success of this informal empire was British sea power, which dominated the coastal communities in the bights of Benin and Biafra. As Palmerston reminded King Kosoko during the Lagos crisis of 1851, ". . . Lagos is near the sea, and . . . on the sea are the ships and cannon of England." No native power faced with the prospects of naval bombardment was ever known to defy the orders of the British government. Until the necessity of defending her interests against the competing nations of Europe arose Britain held on to the cheap informal empire of the period 1830–1884.

In the Delta the transition from an informal to a formal empire was dictated, first, by the needs of a rapidly expanding hinterland trade. A survey of the position in 1878 will reveal the striking progress made since 1832. Four British companies were now operating in the Niger valley—The West African Company (Manchester); Messrs. Alexander Miller Brothers & Co. (Glasgow); The Central African Trading Company (London); and James Pinnock & Co. (Liverpool). This list does not include the several small firms and individual merchants pushing their way up the Delta rivers into the hinterland. Between them these companies employed fourteen steamers in the Niger trade. All maintained trading posts at Akassa, Abo, Ndoni, Abragada, Odogeri, Utchi, Osamari, Alenso, Lower Oko, Onitsha, Gbokem, Lokoja, Yimaha, Egga, and many other posts on the Niger and Benue. The approximate quantity of produce shipped from the Niger valley for the year 1878 was as follows:

5,000 tons of palm oil at £39 a ton		£195,000
65 tons of ivory at £800 a ton		52,000
1,500 tons of shea butter at £39 a ton		58,500
150 tons of beri-seed at £24 a ton		3,600
50 tons of groundnuts at £12 a ton		600
		£309,700

River navigation had been carried to a point 600 miles in the hinterland. Laird's dream had come true and the Nigerian hinterland had been opened to British commerce.

Once again the Foreign Office, in the hinterland as on the coast, had to face the fact that the invasion of the Niger basin by British traders had drawn the mother country irresistibly into the politics of the interior. "Some years ago," wrote Wylde in 1876, "the traders on the African coast were given to understand that if they chose to establish themselves up the rivers where the natives were hostile they must do so at their own responsibility . . . they must . . . not expect to be protected by our cruisers." No one took this injunction seriously. The realization by the British government that sea power was of little use hundreds of miles inland brought to the fore the issue of providing security for internal commerce. "Where there is money to be made," continued Wylde, "our merchants will be certain to intrude themselves, and . . . if they establish a lucrative trade public opinion in this country practically compels us to protect them." Economic opportunity is dependent for its exploitation on political security; this security British merchants lacked in their trade with the interior. The government recognized that to attain success, trade and political frontiers must march hand in hand.

Even in the sixties the consuls from Burton onwards emphasized that with the trade frontier moving fast into the hinterland the island of Fernando Po was no longer suited as the headquarters of their activities. In 1872 Lord Granville approved the transfer of the Consulate to Old Calabar on the mainland. In this movement from the coast to the interior the inland traders did not always wait for the government to protect them. As a rule they pushed their way through the creeks and rivers of the Niger Delta, in armed boats, to the oil markets. The following description of one of these boats owned by a British company will illustrate the general trend: "Messrs. Miller Brothers & Co. have a steamer out here the *Sultan of Socotoo* well armed and having iron screens for protection of those on board; she is . . . useful in establishing factories in unfrequented localities. . . ." Using this steamer to fight their way through Delta opposition, Miller Brothers established factories on the Qua Eboe River, "situated between Opobo and Old Calabar, where they diverted a portion of the trade" from those two city-states. They were eventually driven off by Ja Ja and King Archibong of Old Calabar, the two most powerful chiefs in the area. As the Liverpool coast traders accepted the inevitability of inland trade, the hostility which used to exist between them and the inland traders gradually disappeared. It now became a fight between the European merchants, on the one hand, and the Niger Delta middlemen on the other. In the seventies the word "tapping" was frequently used to describe the activities of the trading steamers which passed above the Delta and intercepted the produce that used to pass through the hands of the middlemen. By 1876 "tapping" had become a regular feature of the Delta trade and with it British "factories" sprang up like mushrooms in the Delta oil markets, formerly a preserve of the middlemen.

From time to time the British government made efforts to provide protection for the expanding commerce of the Niger valley. When native hostility necessitated the evacuation of the interior consulate at Lokoja in 1869, Britain depended partly on her friendship with Masaba, king of Bida, and partly on the warships that ascended the river in the rainy season for the protection of the life and property of her subjects. In 1870 Lieutenant Molyneux went up the Niger in H.M.S. *Pioneer* accompanied by the Lagos government steamer *Eyo*, and paid a visit to King Masaba, who annually received presents and ammunition from the British government for his services. In 1871 a diplomatic agent, Mr. W. H. Simpson, was dispatched by the Foreign Office to report on hinterland trade. He was at Lokoja (center of this trade) from August to October and paid many visits to Masaba, reporting very favorably on the support of this chief for the British cause:

> *I was indeed much struck by the evident loyalty and reverence with which he [Masaba] treated any matter relating to Her Majesty and I am satisfied that the continued maintenance of friendly relations with the British Government and of commercial intercourse with Her Majesty's subjects is the principal object of his desires, as it is the mainstay of his policy at home and the foundation upon which his position and his influence amongst his neighbors unquestionably rests. But his great object is the obtaining of guns and ammunition from the expeditions and thereby maintaining a military superiority over his neighbors.*

Between the years 1871–1879 military expeditions visited the Niger basin annually, destroying Delta and hinterland towns that had attacked British life and property. So long as the warships remained in the vicinity of the trading posts a thriving trade was done; during the seven months of the dry season, when the ships could not ascend the river, Africans resumed their attacks on the invaders. War and trade alternated with the seasons. In some localities, Onitsha for instance, the sustained attack on trading posts and the pillaging of British goods, even in the presence of warships, made trade impossible. In 1879 H.M.S. *Pioneer* removed the £50,000 worth of British trade goods at Onitsha and then subjected the town to naval bombardment for three days. Not content with destroying the section of the town situated on the river bank the British forces "the following day . . . marched to the inner town about 3 miles distant, and burned it; and on the next day we levelled all the walls left standing in the lower town." Consul Easton, who led the operations, concluded: "Our proceedings at Onitsha will have a most salutary effect up and down the Niger, and the missionaries and traders unanimously gave us their thanks for our promptness and decision." The Onitsha affair was not an isolated incident. Yamaha on the Benue, another important inland trading station, was destroyed in the same year for attacking British traders. Idah and Aboh were bombarded and at the latter "several hundreds were killed and the streets were strewn with corpses." British newspapers, especially *The Times,* condemned these atrocities. The Foreign Office, baffled by an unprecedented situation, complained that "it would be impossible for Her Majesty's Government to undertake to protect [British] merchants in every quarter of the globe." They admitted, however, that the economic opportunity offered by the Niger valley was great. "We have opened" the Niger to trade "and the result is a thriving business in many portions of that river." Although no specific plan for imposing its authority on the vast hinterland was devised, the government labored to introduce an "Amended Order-in-Council . . . enabling our Consuls on the West African coast to act magisterially up the different rivers." The political unsettlement which accompanied commercial expansion in the Delta, Iboland, and the Hausa country made trade not only insecure but at times impossible. In 1879, therefore, the problem that confronted the British merchant and official was clear. Trade up the Niger had been proved large and profitable: its peaceful exploitation demanded some form of political security. Without peace and security, trade could not flourish. . . .

The informal control which Britain exercised in the Niger Delta flourished as long as she remained the undisputed master in the Bight of Biafra. There is evidence that the Foreign Office had become suspicious of French activities in the Gulf of Guinea in the period 1880–1885 and was planning to assume more direct and effective control of that part of West Africa. In fact Consul Hewett had been charged with the task of securing a protectorate over the Delta region in 1883. But it took twelve months to give effect to this decision and in the meantime Hewett found himself forestalled at the Cameroons by Bismarck's agent. One is forced to the conclusion that the Consul and the Foreign Office could not have believed the French danger to be imminent. French competition, directed from the base at Porto Novo, was of course always watched, especially in the vicinity of Lagos. From time to time British merchants sent information about French intrigues on the coast to the Foreign Office. But there was little evidence of a concerted move by France to displace the British on the coast of Biafra. In the Cameroons German merchants from Hamburg had always worked on friendly terms with British traders. Not a few became useful members of the Courts of Equity. International rivalry was therefore never acute in the Delta as it was in the hinterland until the unexpected German annexation of the Cameroons in 1884. This brief episode has been the subject of much comment.

On 11 July 1884 the German gunboat *Mowe* anchored off the

Cameroons River. It had on board Gustav Nachtigal, the German Commissioner for West Africa. Bismarck had notified the British Foreign Office of Nachtigal's mission, stating that he was "authorized to conduct, on behalf of the Imperial Government, negotiations connected with certain questions." The commissioner sailed for Africa ostensibly to investigate "the state of German commerce on the coast" and no one realized that Bismarck was about to launch Germany on her career of empire building. This mission had been a closely guarded secret, and Nachtigal, acting under careful instructions from Bismarck, avoided areas of the continent claimed by France. Before his arrival in the Cameroons the ground had been prepared by German traders there aided by the German Consul from Gaboon. As a result of their work, on 14 July 1884 the occupation of the Cameroons became official and German flags were raised in most towns of the new protectorate. . . .

The acquisition of the Cameroons by Germany, a district then dominated by British consular power, soon revealed the inadequacies of the informal methods of control which had served Britain well in the years before 1884. With the emergence of international rivalry it became clear that nothing short of formal annexation would meet the need. The German occupation of the Cameroons therefore marked a definite break in British policy in the Niger Delta.

Armed with the instructions which he received from the Foreign Office on 16 May 1884 and which charged him to secure a British protectorate over the Niger territories, Consul Hewett proceeded with great speed and efficiency to conclude treaties of protection with African states in the bights of Benin and Biafra. Treaty-making on the coast occupied him from 14 July to the end of August 1884. He ascended the rivers Niger and Benue in September and concluded further treaties with chiefs of the interior, most of whom were already under the protection of the National African Company. Before the end of October the countries in the Delta and lower Niger were brought under British protection. It was due to Hewett's work and to the exertions of Sir George Goldie that the British delegates at the Berlin West African Conference of 1885 were able to claim for their country ascendancy over the Delta and the lower Niger.

On the 5th of June 1885 Great Britain declared a protectorate over the Niger districts which comprised "the territories on the line of

coast between the British protectorate of Lagos and the right or western bank of the Rio del Rey," and the "territories on both banks of the
Niger, from its confluence with the river Benue at Lokoja to the sea,
as well as territories on both banks of the river Benue, from the confluence up to and including Ibi." The Niger Coast protectorate was
designed to keep out European rivals. As Vice-Consul Johnston observed: "So long as we keep other European nations out, we need not
be in a hurry to go in."

After 1885 British policy in the Delta gradually became more coherent and consistent. But the "paper protectorate" proclaimed in the
Niger territories had yet to be converted into "effective occupation."
The vague sovereignty bestowed on the great powers over West Africa
by the Berlin Conference was based almost entirely on treaty rights.
The greater number of these treaties were obtained in a questionable
manner. Native chiefs were coerced into signing agreements the provisions of which they never understood. In this way they signed away
their rights, the rights of their people, and their lands, acts which in
strict West African customary law were beyond their competence. As
events were to prove, however, these treaties became inadequate for
the purposes of "effective occupation." Since the chiefs had not volun-
tarily surrendered their territories they resisted the encroachment of
the foreigner with every means in their power to the bitter end. At best
the treaties enabled the competing and invading Europeans to demarcate their spheres of activity in the scramble for African territory. But
it was force that decided the issue. "In the last analysis," said Cook,
"the position of every power in Africa rested on 'effective occupation'
backed by force." The critical years 1885–1900 witnessed the subjuga-
tion and "pacification" of Nigeria by British forces. During these years
the impact of European industrialism, hitherto restricted to the Atlantic
seaboard, rapidly spread to the tribal interior. . . .

Saadia Touval

TREATY-MAKING AND THE SCRAMBLE

Saadia Touval of the University of Jerusalem reviews the policies of treaty-making and border delimitation in this article and describes the role played in the process by various African leaders. The article thus suggests the need for further attention to the African scene and further consideration of the implementation of European diplomacy.

The partition of Africa and the delimitation of its borders are generally considered to have been arbitrary acts, imposed by the European powers without reference to local conditions. Many European writers, until recently, used to view the Africans as simple savages and passive objects of the scramble. Many present-day African nationalists tend to view the African people as the passive victims of the scramble. Thus, although divided on almost everything else, they both seem to agree about the passivity of the Africans in relation to the scramble and the partition. One wonders, however, whether these interpretations correspond to what really happened: were the Africans passive or did they influence the outcome by being involved in the process? . . .

Accepting as a fact that the ultimate decisions on the allocation of disputed territories and the delimitation of borders were always made by Europeans, one is tempted to speculate whether in any way Africans influenced such decisions. If it can be shown that in some cases, even indirectly, Africans did influence such decisions, then, perhaps, the generalization that territories were allocated and borders were drawn without any reference to local conditions may have to be qualified.

A convenient way to examine these questions seems to be through a discussion of the treaties concluded between representatives of European powers and African rulers at the time of the scramble. Such treaties provide us with a connecting thread between the African societies and the European decisions concerning the partition.

From Saadia Touval, "Treaties, Borders, and the Partition of Africa," *Journal of African History* 7 (1966): 279–289, 291–292. Used with permission of *The Journal of African History* and Cambridge University Press.

It is not intended here to examine the moral and legal problems connected with the treaties. The treaties, being part of the process of European colonial expansion, must be judged accordingly. The legal questions are manifold. There were different kinds of treaties—economic and political; some were made by representatives of European governments, and others on behalf of private bodies. The treaties as a whole, and many of their provisions, can be called into question on legal grounds; the sovereign international personality of the signatories can be disputed; it is usually unclear whether the making of the treaties conformed to the constitutional processes of the societies concerned; the powers of the signatories are often questionable; and the territorial limits to which the treaty is supposed to apply are doubtful. Although both the legal and the moral issues concerning the treaties are important and interesting, they fall outside the scope of this essay, which will deal only with the political meaning attached to treaties by Europeans and Africans, and the use made of the treaties by them.

Our discussion will start with a brief examination of some European attitudes to the treaties, which is followed by an analysis of some African attitudes to them. Next, we turn to the effect of treaties upon the territorial settlements and border delimitations. Finally, in conclusion, an attempt will be made to assess the influence of the African involvement upon the partition, and some qualifications will be offered concerning the arbitrariness of the border delimitations.

Let us first turn to the question of what the treaties meant to the Europeans concerned in making them.

European motives for making treaties with African rulers were manifold. Foremost among them was the expectation that such treaties could be used to support claims for international recognition of territorial pretensions.

No doubt a large number of the treaties can be considered fraudulent. Some were forgeries concocted by agents sent to conclude treaties who failed to accomplish their mission. But there is good reason to consider as genuine at least some of the treaties concluded at the time of the scramble.

Since one of the objects of the treaties, from the European point of view, was that they should be used in support of territorial claims in negotiations with rival European powers, the governments concerned

were interested in presenting as convincing an image of the genuineness of their treaties as possible. Treaties invoked in support of a
territorial claim were not always closely scrutinized by the competing
European government, but, when a treaty was subjected to scrutiny
and found wanting, the negotiating position of the government presenting the treaty was seriously weakened.

Conscientious treaty makers therefore used to take elaborate precautions in order to ensure that their treaties were indisputable. The
proper procedure required both translating the treaty and explaining
it to the African signatories through interpreters, and the certification
by witnesses that this had been done. Further precautions, sometimes resorted to, included attempts to ascertain that the signatory
was the real chief or ruler, and not a "straw chief" put up for the
occasion, and also attention to the constitutional and ceremonial
details of the act. Lugard, when trying through treaties to obtain
supplies and facilitate his communications in East Africa, used to
impress upon the Africans the significance of the undertaking by
entering into blood-brotherhood by traditional ceremony with the
principal signatory, in addition to the formal conclusion of the written treaty. . . .

Formal certification that a treaty was translated and explained to
the local ruler did not ensure, of course, that the treaty was really
genuine. Interpreters did not always faithfully explain the treaty to
the Africans. . . .

At the time, European attitudes concerning the genuineness of the
treaties were rather ambivalent. On the one hand, they tended to
doubt and ridicule the propriety of the "treaty game." On the other
hand, they sometimes, perhaps too seldom, took the treaties seriously, considering that the treaties imposed upon them also some
obligations. The French review *Politique Coloniale* expressed the
doubter's point of view when it exclaimed at the time of the exasper-
ating Anglo-French negotiations on Nikki: "And what, in any case,
is the value of these scraps of paper which are triumphantly brought
back by all the travellers who take the trouble to ask for them?"

More balanced doubts were expressed by Lugard when he noted
in his diary the reasons why he refrained from using the treaty forms
he was given when he made a treaty with Eiyeki (Waiyaki), a Kikuyu
chief:

> *I now presented him with a flag, and explained its use. I also made a treaty, but as I do not believe in the printed treaty forms of the Company by which a man gives all his land and rights of rule to the Company in exchange of their "Govt. and protection," I made out my own treaty form. This Company's treaty is an utter fraud. No man if he understood would sign it, and to say that a savage chief has been told that he cedes all rights to the Company in exchange for nothing is an obvious untruth. If he has been told that the Company will protect him against his enemies, and share in his wars as an Ally, he has been told a lie, for the Comp. have no idea of doing any such thing and no force to do it with if they wished.*

Implicit in Lugard's criticism of the standard treaty forms, and in the special treaty he formulated, is the feeling that the treaty is a mutual obligation.

In any event, whether for reasons of self-interest or otherwise, at least some of the treaties were made in such a manner as to ensure that they be regarded as genuine.

What did the treaties mean to the Africans? Considering that the treaties often stipulated the cession of rights and acceptance of European "protection," and that they were often translated and explained to the Africans, one is bound to ask why African rulers entered into such compacts.

One possible explanation is that they were coerced. The coercive measures may have been the explicit threat of superior force. This apparently was the situation when the ruler of the Mossi, newly installed by the French after their military victory which led to the deposition of the former ruler who refused to acknowledge their protection, signed a protectorate treaty with France. In other cases, even when no superior force was in evidence, an implied threat of force may have played a role in the adherence of African rulers to treaties. Yet, it would seem that the actual use of force, or a threat of force, played a role relatively rarely. The Europeans' agents normally travelled with only a light escort, and the actual power relationship at the time and place the treaty was signed was often in the African ruler's favor. Nevertheless, it can still be assumed that a measure of coercion might have played a role, as the Europeans' mere reputation for power might have sufficed to overawe the African ruler.

Probably, in a great number of cases, the European emissaries obtained their treaties through the combined effect of coercion and inducement, the stick and the carrot. We can view such methods of persuasion as ranging from cases in which the implied threat of punishment in the event of refusal was preponderant, to cases in which the carrot was the major inducement, while the possibility of punishment by European power in the event of refusal seemed to the African ruler remote and unlikely.

The inducements offered in soliciting treaties varied. Sometimes, sovereignty was ceded in return for goods or money, such as the cession of the small island of Mussa by the Sultan of Tajura to the British East India Company for the price of ten bags of rice. More frequently, probably, the inducements were not merely economic, but also political and military in nature. Thus Lobengula, the Matabele ruler, granted the Rudd Concession for exclusive mineral rights in return for a monthly subsidy of £100, one thousand breech-loading guns, and an armed steamboat on the Zambezi. The Royal Niger Company apparently obtained many of its treaties among the pagan peoples of northern Nigeria through the combined inducements of lucrative subsidies and a promise of protection from Fulani conquest. A more elaborate argument was presented by Lugard to Sekgoma, chief of the Tawana in Ngamiland. In return for Sekgoma's agreement to revise the terms of a mineral concession which had been granted to the British West Charterland Company, Lugard offered on behalf of the company to support his boundary claims against the rival British South Africa Company, and to advise him in his delicate relations with the latter. Lugard also gave him some modest presents—a writing case, and notepaper stamped "Ngamiland." The prospects of extensive political and military benefit probably induced the emir of Muri, on the Benue, to agree to a protectorate treaty with France.

It may be argued that, despite the translation and explanation of the treaties, the African chiefs did not fully grasp their meaning. No doubt many chiefs signed treaties they did not understand. But, as there were chiefs who refused to make a treaty, and others who signed only after pressure or persuasion, we can assume that the meaning of the undertaking was not beyond their comprehension. Many chiefs must have been aware that by attaching their signature to the paper produced by the white man they were signifying the establishment of some new relationship with him, different from the relationship which had existed hitherto. African rulers in the interior were not acquainted with European political institutions and diplomatic practice. But this does not mean that they were politically innocent. African societies did not exist in a political vacuum, and their leaders usually had political experience gained in dealing with neighboring societies, with tribal authorities that were superior or subordinate to them, and with rival groups or individuals. Therefore they were aware of some possible implications and uses of their newly created relationship with the white man. Thus, when European emissaries came and offered various inducements in return for treaties, their offers often fell upon politically sensitized ears. Although, probably, most African rulers did not fully comprehend the meaning of the treaties, they felt their political significance, and often tried to take advantage of the inducements offered. . . .

The political benefits African rulers hoped to obtain, and sometimes actually obtained, through treaties varied. Some, such as the Yoruba ruler of Kishi, hoped that the treaty would help them preserve a precarious status quo, vis-à-vis pressures from Africans and Europeans alike. Others may have had more far-reaching plans of taking advantage of their European alliance to strengthen their position in conflicts of long standing with rival African rulers. Mandara, chief of Moshi in Chaggaland, had apparently great hopes concerning the benefits of his association with Sir Harry Johnston. Another African polity which used its alliance with a European power to the best of its advantage, for the extension and enhancement of its influence, was Buganda.

One of the early Buganda attempts to make its treaty relationship with Britain serve its own interests was Kabaka Mwanga's demand that his treaty with Lugard should explicitly state that the tributary states would continue to pay tribute to him. European alliances also served the opposite purpose of throwing off a superior's yoke. . . . On other occasions, African rulers concluded treaties with Europeans in the hope of obtaining protection against slave raiders. . . .

Sometimes African rulers played the delicate political game of trying to preserve as much of their independence as possible, by playing off the European powers against each other. Thus, when the emir of Yola felt threatened by the French expedition led by Lt. Mizon, he appealed to the Royal Niger Company for protection, and later also reluctantly signed a treaty with the company. But shortly thereafter, probably hoping thus to reduce the company's interference, he signed a treaty with the French as well. Similar hopes of reducing British influence, in this case by enlisting the Germans, probably motivated Mwanga's invitation to Emin Pasha in 1891 to come and visit his country. An assessment of alternative European orientations, undoubtedly influenced by Sir Harry Johnston's explanation of them, induced Arab rulers on Lake Nyasa to conclude treaties with Britain.

One of the more comprehensive advantages derived by an African ruler from a European alliance is demonstrated by the treaty concluded between the emir of Muri, on the Benue, and the French emissary, Lt. Mizon. The emir was presented with a gift of arms. Mizon's men fought on the emir's side in a war against a neighboring people who had been his traditional enemies. The treaty with France also helped the emir to resist pressure from the Royal Niger Company, which was apparently trying to undermine his authority among some of his vassals.

What has been implied in some of the previous examples should perhaps be emphasized: on occasion the initiative for treaties came from Africans, who sought the protection of certain European powers against what seemed to them at the time a much greater evil. In addition to the examples cited already, one may mention the Somalis, in what subsequently became British Somaliland, who sought British protection against Ethiopian attempts to extend their authority into areas used by them for grazing. Another example is the Mogho Naba Wadogo, the Mossi ruler, who, after being defeated by the French, appealed in 1897–1898 to the British for protection, invoking a treaty he had signed with a British agent in 1894.

All this should of course not be taken to imply that the Africans were in any way pleased with the situation in which they found themselves. The situation was not of their making, and often not to their liking. But what I hope the above analysis does demonstrate is that they were not passive victims, but were rather trying to make the most of a difficult situation.

However, probably only a few were as far-sighted as Lobengula, whose predicament is eloquently described in a passage quoted by Mason. It is a description of how Lobengula was at a certain point so hard pressed both internally and externally that he appeared likely to welcome a British alliance. And he concluded such an alliance, while at the same time tragically predicting its disastrous consequences, likening England to a chameleon, gradually preparing to get at a fly, and himself to the fly which is ultimately swallowed by the chameleon.

At this stage, it is right that we should ask what was the effect of such treaties upon the territorial settlements which resulted from the scramble.

To avoid misunderstanding, it should be stated that, only when a European power concerned decided so, were treaties taken into consideration in connection with the territorial settlements. Sometimes such a European decision to take into account or invoke a treaty between itself and some African ruler was prompted or influenced by an appeal by the Africans concerned. Yet the decision whether a treaty should be taken into consideration was ultimately a European one.

In trying to evaluate the effect of the treaties upon the territorial settlements, we shall limit our discussion to disputed territories and frontier regions. At the same time, however, we should recognize that, in the case of territories that were not in dispute at the end of the nineteenth century, treaties concluded there probably helped to win general recognition of the primacy of respective European powers in these territories, and thus that the treaties played a partial role in determining territorial allocations.

When a European government referred to treaties concluded with African rulers in support of its territorial claims, its argument was usually twofold: that it had acquired rights through the treaty, and that it had entered into obligations toward an African people which it could not honorably relinquish. Both arguments can, of course, be questioned. The native ruler often did not fully comprehend the nature of the rights which by the treaty he conferred. And the European power often did not intend to fulfill the obligations which it undertook. The reference to the treaties by European governments can therefore be regarded as hypocritical. But the important point here is that treaties were often resorted to in justification of territorial claims.

In the territorial negotiations between European powers, treaties were useful in conferring bargaining advantages. One kind of a bar-

gaining advantage was that treaties endowed territories with exchange value. A territory in which a power had obtained a treaty
could be "ceded" to another power in return for a counter-concession. Claims to territories in which no treaties were concluded, or
where such treaties were contested as faulty, were considered weak.
The value of the concession of abandoning such weak claims was
much smaller, and the counter-concession which could be elicited
from the rival power was such as the rival considered commensurate.

Sometimes a territory claimed by one power by virtue of a treaty
was subsequently occupied by a rival. But the rights which the first
power obtained by the treaty could still be used for bargaining
purposes. The British treaty with the ruler of Mossi is an example.
As already mentioned, the Mossi ruler fled to British territory after
being defeated and deposed by France, and asked Britain to assist
him to regain his position. Such assistance was not granted. But the
treaty with him was a card in Britain's hand in the negotiations with
France in 1898.

Another kind of bargaining advantage was derived from treaties
in border negotiations. The limits of a territory claimed could sometimes be extended by reference to the borders of an African polity
towards which the power claiming the disputed territory had entered
into treaty obligations. One example of such a situation, the results
of which are evident on the map, is the deflection of the Kenya-
Tanganyika border near Mount Kilimanjaro. In that region, it was
agreed between Britain and Germany in 1886, and subsequently
confirmed in 1890, that the border between their respective spheres
would pass "midway between Taveta and Chagga." The line thus
respected British rights to Taveta, which rested at that time upon
the treaty concluded there by Sir Harry Johnston, whereas the German claim to Chagga rested on Karl Peters's treaties. The Anglo-
French agreement of 1890, delimiting their respective spheres on
the Niger, stated that the British sphere will include "all that fairly
belongs to the Kingdom of Sokoto," with which the Royal Niger
Company claimed a treaty. . . . The border between Nigeria and
Dahomey, as agreed between Britain and France in 1898, also contained deflections to take account of treaties between Britain and
African rulers. To cite another example: in 1904, as part of a
comprehensive settlement between England and France, the line

which is now the border between Nigeria and Niger was amended so as to include the territories of the sultanates of Tessawa and Maradi and Zinder, with which France had treaties, within the French sphere.

A territorial settlement in which the territorial limits of an African polity were accorded great significance was the delimitation of the border between Angola and Northern Rhodesia. In 1891 it was agreed between Britain and Portugal that a section of the border between their respective possessions in Central Africa would follow the western border of the Barotse kingdom. However a difficulty soon developed, as the two sides disagreed about the westward extent of that kingdom's territories. In 1903 the dispute was submitted to the arbitration of the king of Italy. His award and definition of the westward limit of the Barotse kingdom was based upon an assessment of the territorial extent of the effective authority of the Barotse ruler.

Of course, a European government invoking in territorial negotiations treaty obligations toward Africans acted in its own interest. But it considered it in its own interest in such cases to try to preserve the territorial integrity of African polities. In this way, therefore, indigenous African political circumstances indirectly influenced border delimitations. . . .

If the Africans were not the passive objects of the partition, but if their relationships with Europeans played a role in the process, then we may have to qualify our views concerning the arbitrariness of the partition. If by "arbitrary" we mean that the final decisions on how to divide the continent and delimit the borders were made by European governments, then the commonly accepted view about the arbitrariness of the process remains valid. But we should be on guard not to accept uncritically the generalization, which is widely taken as an implication of the above, that the borders were drawn by European statesmen, assisted by draftsmen, in complete disregard of African realities and local circumstances. It has been estimated that approximately 30 per cent of the total length of African borders follow straight lines. Such straight lines can be assumed to have been decided upon in complete disregard of local needs and circumstances. This leaves about 70 per cent of the total length of African borders which do not follow straight lines, and which were defined mostly in terms of geographical features. Such definition of borders does not preclude the possibility that consideration of local circumstances influenced the decisions on the location of the border.

We have seen above that treaties were used in support of territorial claims, and that frontiers of African polities were sometimes incorporated into European-drawn borders. . . . Therefore the disregard of indigenous political circumstances was not universal.

A few examples, chosen at random, seem to indicate that on some occasions considerations regarding the local economy and communications were taken into account.

Among the more interesting attempts to find suitable borders between the newly acquired European possessions in Africa was the mission of Sir Harry Johnston to the Rio del Rey area in 1887 with a view to finding a suitable river to mark the border between the British and German spheres. Johnston's recommendation, resulting from the survey, was that a small stream by the name of Ndiang be selected, since it formed an ethnic as well as an economic boundary. Another example of a boundary recommended on the basis of a local survey was the line between Uganda and the Sudan. The boundary proposed by Col. J. R. L. Macdonald was considered by him to constitute the commercial watershed between the Nile route and the Uganda Railway route. Again, misapprehension of Uganda's external communications apparently influenced the decision to have it administered separately from the East Africa protectorate, and led in 1902 to the transfer of what was Uganda's eastern province to Kenya. Thirdly, the ludicrous shape of the Caprivi strip is the result of Anglo-German agreement that German South-West Africa should have free access to the Zambezi, which people believed at that time would become an important communication route between the interior and the Indian Ocean. Finally, communication problems of the French administration between the Niger and Zinder brought about the rectification of the Niger-Nigeria border by the Anglo-French agreement of 1904.

Some territorial agreements included specific provision for subsequent modification in the light of local requirements. The task of examining local conditions was usually assigned to a demarcation commission, which surveyed the border and marked it on the ground. Modifications recommended by such commissions were of a

minor nature, but they nevertheless constituted an attempt to take
local conditions into account and thus to diminish the arbitrariness
of the border.

Such delimitations of borders may have been wrong. The criterion
for selecting a border might have been a bad one, or it might have
misapplied, or the decisions might have been based on erroneous
information. But the facts to be noted are that attempts were occasionally made to take local conditions into account, that the decisions often involved a choice between alternatives, and that the
choices and decisions were often reasoned and considered ones.
All this does not mean that the borders were good ones; but perhaps
they are not as arbitrary as they are often supposed to be.

We have not set out to prove that African borders in toto were not
arbitrarily drawn. But we hope to have given sufficient reason why
the generalization that the Africans were passive objects in the
process, and that local conditions were disregarded, seems untenable. No doubt the problem deserves careful study in the light of
archive material. Furthermore, comparison with the processes by
which borders were delimited in Europe, and elsewhere, may help
to place the partition of Africa in a better perspective.

John D. Hargreaves
WEST AFRICAN STATE REACTIONS
TO THE SCRAMBLE

*Professor of history in the University of Aberdeen, Scotland, John Hargreaves
has been a careful student of modern West African affairs and has written
many studies on the subject, of which his* Prelude to the Partition of West
Africa *(1963) is the most significant. In the article reproduced below, he
further elaborated some of the ideas he suggested in his "Towards a History
of the Partition" (1960), in which he argued that historians should treat nineteenth century African states as other than "museum pieces."*

Reprinted by permission of the Cambridge University Press, from John D. Hargreaves,
"West African States and the European Conquest," in L. H. Gann and Peter Duignan,
eds., *The History and Politics of Colonialism, 1870–1914*, Vol. I of *Colonialism in
Africa, 1870–1960* (Cambridge, 1969), pp. 199–202, 205–216.

A common though superficial view of the partition of Africa is that Europeans, having decided to impose their power, proceeded to do so, enabled by the superior technology represented by Belloc's famous maxim gun. J. S. Keltie, author of the earliest and still the most detailed general account, believed that "we have seen the bulk of the one barbarous continent parcelled out among the most civilized powers of Europe." In such a perspective, European occupation inaugurated such a radically new phase in African history that the methods and motivations of the conquerors seemed a vastly more important subject for study than the reactions of the conquered.

From the new frontier of African historical studies, the view is rather different. We can trace how, in the centuries before the partition, African states, entering into more or less stable relations, grew or diminished in power as a result of commerce, statecraft, war and internal changes. The nineteenth century provided in Africa many examples of what philosophic historians might earlier have called "great revolutions . . . and the rise and fall of states." One may see what has been described as a sort of African partition of Africa, a radical reshaping of political structures and boundaries, taking place throughout the century. It is most evident in the Muslim countries of the western Sudan, with the great Fulani jihad in Sokoto, the consolidation of Bornu, the rise and defeat of Macina, the foundation of the Tukulor state of El Hadj 'Omar and later of the military empires of Samory (Samori) and Rabeh. But in coastal areas, too, many peoples were adapting their attitudes and institutions in response to the challenges presented by foreign traders, missionaries and governors. Wolof states took to peanut-growing and to Islam; the Fon state in Dahomey reorganized its economy and extended its power; the "city-states" of the Oil Rivers perfected their mechanisms for controlling trade.

Not all such states were completely wiped from the map by European imperialism. Although some, like the Muslim empires that faced the French military in Haut-Sénégal-Niger, were deliberately broken up by the conquerors, the cultural identity, institutional structure and ruling personnel of others survived not only under colonial rule but after its termination. The Tolon Na, a traditional Dagomba chief, represented Nkrumah's radical republic of Ghana in Lagos; the ancient dynasty of Mossi played active if somewhat conservative roles in Voltaic politics during the 1940s and 1950s; rulers of small Mende and Temne chiefdoms provided much of the basis for the rule of the Sierra Leone People's Party. Most striking of all was the power wielded within the Nigerian federation by representatives of the ruling houses of the Fulani empire. It is therefore relevant to many present problems to inquire how such survivals became possible, what forces or conditions determined whether African states could retain their identity, what characteristics were needed for survival through the violent mutations induced by the European partition.

Historians of colonial policy might propose a simple hypothesis: that the decisive factor was the policy and attitudes of the occupying powers, whose material superiority was such that they could reshape the continent in accordance with their national interests and ideologies. British governors and consuls, their activities watched on the one hand by ministries drilled in the need to economize by administrative improvisation, and on the other by merchants anxious not to damage potential customers too badly, were unable to press so severely upon the African states that confronted them as ambitious French *militaires,* shrugging off civilian control as they sought Napoleonic conquests. One mode of expansion pointed towards the pragmatic philosophy of indirect rule, the other towards an integrationist ideal attainable only after French control had imposed rigorous processes of levelling and indoctrination. . . .

Much is no doubt explained by these contrasting attitudes; and certainly in the longer run administrative policies and doctrines developed which made it far easier for African political structures to survive, and even harden, under British rule than under French rule. . . . While British practitioners of indirect rule were led to revive political institutions which their predecessors had destroyed —or even, as in Iboland, to create state structures that earlier generations of Africans apparently neglected to develop for themselves—the French tended increasingly to turn chieftaincy into a bureaucratic hierarchy of subordinate *fonctionnaires*.

But in the earlier period, while the partition of West Africa was still taking place, the contrast between French and British policies was far less absolute. The British were led by the circumstances of their incursion to destroy many historic states as political entities, to acquiesce in the arbitrary partition of others. . . . Indeed, throughout the nineteenth century British attitudes towards African authority were by no means consistent. The interest which many saw in identifying and strengthening "strong native governments" as collaborators in the policies of "informal empire" was in practice largely neutralized by pressures arising out of local interests and commitments, or evangelical impulses to remold the continent more nearly in Britain's image.

Towards Ashanti (Asante), for example, British officials from time to time advocated policies of coexistence and collaboration with a state which seemed to be capable of bringing tranquility and ordered market conditions to an extensive area of the Gold Coast hinterland. Yet Britain's position in and commitments to the coastal states led to repeated conflicts, strengthening an antithetical stereotype of "a savage and barbarous power . . . a constant menace to the safety of the Gold Coast Colony . . . a formidable hindrance to its development and the advance of civilization . . . an obstacle to trade, and . . . a disgrace to humanity."

By January 1896 fears of advancing French influence in the Sudan, pressure from British and Gold Coast merchants interested in trade with the interior, and the failure of some half-hearted and unskillful attempts to establish a form of supervisory control led Joseph Chamberlain to authorize a military expedition. Although Prempeh, the Asantehene, offered no military resistance, his failure to satisfy inflated demands for a gold indemnity provided the occasion for his deposition and exile, and the establishment of a British protectorate in which the member states of the confederacy were placed under the direct supervision of the resident. Here as elsewhere British attitudes towards African states seem to have been determined with characteristic British pragmatism.

But Frenchmen could be pragmatists too, quite prepared to maintain such African political structures as might fit in with their short-term programs. This, on the whole, happened more frequently in coastal districts, where civilian officials and commerical interests could more effectively check the belligerence of military officers, and where the need to forestall the British led French officials to conclude protectorate treaties with chiefs whose territories they were not yet ready to occupy physically. . . .

Comparisons between French and British policies need to be

taken no further in this discussion. Neither side embarked on the occupation of its African empire with a fixed and monolithic policy, pointing towards a single inevitable fate for the African polities in its path. If the aims and aspirations of those Europeans who led the advance sometimes implied a need for military conquest, more often they were such as could be satisfied by some form of treaty providing access to commercial markets, denying land to rival imperialisms, laying foundations for political control. . . .

Given this range of possible attitudes on the part of the European invaders, a number of options might be open to African rulers. Among the short-term advantages obtainable from treaties or from collaboration with Europeans were not merely access to fire-arms and consumer goods, but opportunities to enlist powerful allies in external or internal disputes. Why then did so many African states reject such opportunities, choosing to resist the Europeans in battle? In West Africa, as in East and Central Africa, it cannot be said that those who opted for resistance were less far-sighted or forward-looking than the "collaborators." In fact they were often the same men. Wobogo, for example, first received Binger cordially; became much more suspicious of the French after his accession; but only fought them after the Voulet mission had made their hostility unmistakably clear. Lat-Dior, *damel* of Cayor, a Senegalese kingdom with much longer experience of the French, was a "modernizer" in his acceptance of commercial groundnut production, and adjustment to its social consequences. After resisting Faidherbe's attempts to replace him by a more compliant ruler, he cooperated with succeeding governors on the more generous terms they offered, but finally reached the sticking-point when the French began to build a railway through his country. Convinced (rightly) that this "steamship on dry land" would erode his sovereignty, he chose to die resisting in 1886. (His name, and reputation, however, live on in the Senegalese army barracks in Dakar.)

Examples could be multiplied indefinitely. Nearly all West African states made some attempt to find a basis on which they could coexist with Europeans. Virtually all seem to have had some interests which they would defend by resistance or revolt—some conception of what can only be described as a rudimentary "national cause" anterior to, and distinct from, the national loyalties demanded by modern independent states. An analysis of the "national cause" of any specific people would need to embrace some values deeply rooted in their own culture and not very readily comprehensible to outsiders, together with some that can be universally understood— claims to territory, freedom to settle matters of internal concern without foreign interference. On this basis they would face the problem of relations with foreigners. Whether it was judged necessary to defend the national cause in battle, and at what stage, depended on variables on both sides of the Afro-European relationship—on African statecraft as well as on European intentions.

In countries where African political structures had already been deeply affected by the growth of export trade, Afro-European relationships were conditioned by economic change. In the Niger delta, among the Yoruba, in coastal areas near Sierra Leone or on the Ivory Coast, political authority was diffused, and many African rulers were moved by considerations of commercial advantage or profit. Studies of "conjuncture" may be needed to explain not only the pressures behind the European advance, but certain African reactions. Trading chiefs and heads of houses, as well as European merchants, sought to maintain the rate of profit in times of falling produce prices. The present discussion approaches the study of African resistance chiefly through rather simple cases, where centralized monarchies possessing the physical means of resistance defended national causes that can be described in fairly simple terms. . . .

One of the classical cases of military resistance seems to be that of Samory, who between 1891 and 1898 fought the French with remarkable tenacity and military skill. Yet the record of his relations with France and Britain in the preceding decade shows many examples of his readiness to negotiate bases for genuine cooperation with either or both, provided that such bases safeguarded certain fundamentals of his independence. His early contacts with the French, beginning with the armed conflict at Keniera in February 1882, were indeed characterized by mutual mistrust and antagonism. But the French had to act circumspectly while building up their military force in the Niger valley, and it was only in early 1885 that Commander A. V. A. Combes's invasion of Bouré (whose gold was so important to Samory's economy) revealed prematurely the full extent of their hostility.

Samory's response was to develop his contacts with the British in Sierra Leone, first established in 1879–1880. After occupying Falaba in 1884, he sent emissaries to Freetown to invite the governor "to ask the Queen to take the whole of his country under her protection." The purpose of the offer was clearly to obtain British support in warding off the French, and Governor Rowe was doubtless correct in interpreting it as a diplomatic flourish not intended to alienate sovereignty. More intent on protecting Sierra Leone's sphere of commercial and political influence among Temnes and Limbas than in seeking influence on the Niger, he did not even report the offer to London until a year later. His reply to Samory was amicable but cool, simply welcoming his promise to respect Temne country—"the Queen's garden"—and agreeing to develop friendly relations and trade.

Yet this was not without importance for Samory. Commercial contacts alone gave him a vital interest in collaboration with Freetown. Until 1892, when the Sierra Leone government enforced the licensing of arms sales according to the Brussels convention of 1890, this route provided Samory with his supply of modern breach-loading rifles, which he was increasingly aware might be needed for use against the French.

Even now, Samory had not accepted armed conflict with France as inevitable. He was not leading a jihad against all Christians, nor a Pan-African revolt against imperialism. He was concerned, practically, with governing and extending the empire he had conquered, with controlling its resources of gold, agricultural produce and men (including, of course, its slaves) and with enforcing the observance of Islam. It was perhaps less evident in the 1880s than later that these conditions were incompatible with the purposes of the French forces on the Niger. French relations with the Tukulor empire of Ségou remained somewhat ambivalent until 1890; and the French military, desperately anxious to forestall supposed British ambitions and chafing under restraint from Paris, were reduced to signing treaties with Samory also.

In March 1886, when Colonel L. L. Frey was obliged to divert his forces against Mamadou Lamina, Samory was able to make a French mission under Captain Tournier modify the terms which they had intended to impose upon him. He secured French recognition not only of his territories on the right bank of the Niger, but of his rights over the contested districts of Bouré and Kangaba. This left him more independence of action than the French were prepared to tolerate; and the following year, J. S. Gallieni (of all the French commanders the one most susceptible to the idea of protectorate relationships with Muslim rulers) sent Captain E. Péroz to negotiate new terms. Samory, although reluctant to damage his prestige by surrendering territory, wished to avoid further battles against French military power at a time when he was about to attack his archenemy Tiéba, chief of Sikasso. After discussion he therefore agreed, by a treaty of 23 March 1887, to abandon the gold of Bouré to the French and to accept a boundary line on the Tinkisso River. According to the French, he agreed also to place his state and any future acquisitions under their protection.

As is often the case with such treaties of protection, it is difficult to tell how far Samory was aware of having entered into some new relationship with France under the protectorate clause. Certainly he interpreted it quite differently from the French (whose immediate concern was not to define their permanent status in his territories, but to acquire a legal title against the British). There is some evidence that Samory believed that the French had undertaken to assist him to further his own designs, in particular against Tiéba; counting on the alliance, he asked Binger for troops and artillery to help in his siege of Sikasso. But he certainly did not regard himself as having made an irreversible surrender of sovereignty. When the French refused to assist him, began to encroach on his territory, and tried to prevent his trading with Freetown, Samory "began to doubt whether, after all, the white man's word could be thoroughly relied upon" and tried, somewhat naively perhaps, to reverse his policy.

There still seemed to be possibilities of balancing British against French. In May 1888 Samory, while still besieging Sikasso, was visited by Major A. M. Festing, an official from Sierra Leone. This devout, garrulous and pompous man had exaggerated faith in his personal powers of persuasion and influence. He had an unrealistic vision of Samory, with Festing as adviser, making peace with his enemies, consolidating his dominions into a genuinely united kingdom, and admitting the railway which the house of F. and A. Swanzy hoped to build from Freetown. Samory was interested, accepted the principle of a railway, and promised to sign a treaty when he returned to Bissandougou; but he refused to risk provoking a French attack before defeating Sikasso. In February 1889, indeed, he signed a new treaty with the French, accepting the Niger as the frontier everywhere and agreeing to direct trade towards French ports; but soon afterwards he returned this treaty (though not that of 1887) to the French. He told another British travelling commissioner that he now considered himself free of obligations and ready to place his people and country under British protection; and on 24 May 1890 he signed a treaty promising not to alienate territory nor undertake obligations to third powers except through the British government. It was, however, too late. London had already decided that the French protectorate treaties must be recognized, that war with France for West Africa was excluded, and had agreed with France on a partition of influence through the middle of Samory's empire. G. H. Garrett's treaty was not ratified, and Samory's partisans in Freetown tried in vain to persuade the government to work with him.

Samory's diplomacy was thus doomed to failure by the constant hostility of most French soldiers. Although some civilians wanted to avoid, or at least defer, a conflict, the ambitious and thrusting Colonel Archinard was hostile to any policy of tolerating Muslim empires. In April 1891 he again slipped the long rein of civilian control and attacked Kankan, intending to cut Samory's supply route to Sierra Leone. Thus the final period of armed resistance began. Until all of Yves Person's work has been published, assessment of Samory's personality and achievements can only be tentative. His dealings with the French were so marked by mutual mistrust and cultural incompatibility that a sober judgment is difficult; but it seems that Samory's attempts at coexistence were at least as seriously intended as those of the Frenchmen with whom he was dealing. For both sides, collaboration involved accepting restrictions of their rights, interests and prestige which came to seem intolerable.

Samory's case thus hardly supports the view of Professors Oliver and Fage that, "nothing was to be gained by resistance and much by negotiation"; nothing that he held important could have been permanently gained by either method. . . .

On the other hand, resistance—if combined at other times with willingness to accommodate and skill in doing so—could further the cause of national survival. In northern Nigeria, most evidently, the military resistance of the emirs did much to determine the basis of the very special relationship which their successors enjoyed with the British administration. Even here, however, D. J. M. Muffett has argued that the conflict of 1903 was due less to intransigent resistance by Sultan Attahiru than to Lugard's determination that, before the British could utilize the Fulani as a "ruling caste," the military basis of British suzerainty should be asserted by conquest. Muffett cites reports by Burdon and Temple to show that before the expedition to Kano and Sokoto Lugard was receiving "a mounting tale of evidence of the Sultan's readiness to be amenable and of the ripeness of the time for a diplomatic approach"; and he questions the translation and the dating of the famous assertion by Attahiru's predecessor that "Between you and us there are no dealings except as between Mussulmans and unbelievers—War, as God Almighty has enjoined on us." Lugard may indeed have hoped the conquest of Kano would make that of Sokoto unnecessary. But as Attahiru saw British soldiers invading his provinces from the south, as he was joined by the stream of Tijaniyya fugitives from the French in the west, it must have seemed increasingly clear that "the doings of the Europeans" threatened the independence of Muslim Africa. It was left for his successors to discover how much could be preserved by collaboration with the British conquerors.

Ashanti, faced with ambivalent British attitudes touched on above, may have missed opportunities of profiting by a more flexible diplomacy. Even hostile officials like W. Brandford Griffith presented a less formidable menace to African autonomy than did Combes or Archinard. Anglo-Ashanti relations have been described as "a mutual and protracted misunderstanding between peoples with fundamentally different conceptual frameworks." The freedom which British imperialists claimed to be bringing to the peoples of Ashanti was not the freedom demanded by the resisters of 1900—freedom "to buy and sell slaves as in the old time," freedom "from demands for carriers

. . . ," "from the obligations of building houses and supplying thatch," and from the unwelcome attentions of "huxters and strangers."

Yet contradictions of this sort, which existed along the whole front of Afro-European relations, did not inevitably have to be resolved by head-on conflict. Might not Prempeh have preserved more of Ashanti political and cultural autonomy by accepting, for example, Griffith's unauthorized protectorate of 1891? He would have preserved the unity of the confederacy, its right to levy customary revenue, and some at least of the "habits and customs of the country"; and although the Asantehene would in many respects, no doubt, have become increasingly dependent on the British resident who was to be appointed, an adaptable Asantehene would doubtless have made the residency equally dependent upon his own collaboration. In retrospect Prempeh's decision that "Ashanti must remain independent as of old" seems to have led logically on to his own deposition in 1896, to Governor Hodgson's ill-advised claim in 1900 to assume the authority of the Golden Stool, and so to the final military conflict and the subjection of Ashanti to direct British administration.

Yet this was by no means the end of the Ashanti nation. In 1900 some of the outlying peoples of the confederacy, who had not always been noted for their loyal support of ruling Asantehenes, rallied to defend Ashanti against British aggression. Prempeh in exile became a more powerful focus of unity than he had been in Kumasi; British administrators in Ashanti, cherishing their separate status under the governor of the Gold Coast, came better to appreciate the strength and complexity of Ashanti national feeling. The advice of R. S. Rattray, appointed as government anthropologist in the 1900s, furthered this reassessment. Ashanti began to seem a natural theatre for experiments in indirect rule. In 1924 Prempeh returned to the country; in 1926 he was recognized as Omanhene of Kumasi. The confederacy was restored under his nephew in 1935, and in 1943 crown lands in Kumasi were restored to the Asantehene. One may reasonably ask whether, but for the resistance of the 1890s, Nkrumah's Convention People's Party would, over fifty years later, have faced such strenuous opposition from the National Liberation Movement, ". . . a Kumasi-centered Ashanti movement, which appealed for support in the name of the Asantehene, the Golden Stool, Ashanti interests, Ashanti history and Ashanti rights." References to military exploits against the British enabled the Ashanti to counter the anti-imperialist centralism of the Convention People's Party with claims to having been anti-imperialist from the first hour. In the long run, something was after all gained by resistance for the Ashanti "national," if not for that of a future unitary Ghanaian nation.

This conclusion is reinforced by a comparison of the experience of the Fon and the Gun during the French occupation of Dahomey. The Fon state of Abomey throughout the nineteenth century exhibited attitudes of proud resistance towards all European attempts to encroach upon its sovereign rights or to compel changes in a way of life which Europeans found particularly abhorrent. This does not imply that it was "hostile to modernization." King Gezo, although unable to meet fully British demands that he should cease exporting slaves and conducting the sacrificial "customs," did much to encourage and participate in the production and sale of palm oil as soon as Europeans showed interest in buying it. But although trade and diplomatic intercourse were welcome, the Dahomeans were uncomfortably aware that Europeans who entered African states to trade sometimes ended by ruling. Thus in 1876, Gelele preferred to undergo a British naval blockade rather than admit European interference in a commercial dispute which lay within his own jurisdiction. Yet he was anxious to avoid a military conflict, for "he who makes the power wins the battle." When the French sent troops to Cotonou under a treaty of cession of 1878 (made in Gelele's name but probably without his consent), he confined himself to obstruction and protests.

Rulers of the Gun kingdom of Porto Novo were more ready to cooperate with Europeans, both politically and commercially. In part, this attitude reflected fear of Abomey, whose armies for much of the nineteenth century constituted an intermittent threat to this smaller Aja state; in part it was caused by the desire of one of the ruling lineages to secure external support for its dynastic and territorial claims. In 1862 King Soji made an unsuccessful attempt to preserve these interests through a French protectorate. After 1874 his son, King Tofa, revived this policy. Tofa was a shrewd politician who worked with European traders to increase his wealth and power; "his succession," say the traditional historians of Porto Novo, "marked the transition into modern times." At first the French could do little to protect his territories against either Abomey or British Lagos, and Tofa showed bitter disappointment with the protectorate. But when Behanzin, who succeeded Gelele at the end of 1889, took more active steps to enforce his territorial claims, the French government was drawn somewhat hesitantly into military operations against him, largely through the intrigues of their ally Tofa.

How did Tofa, the "collaborator," fare by comparison with Behanzin, "the shark that troubled the bar"? Although Behanzin defended Dahomean rights more vigorously than Gelele had latterly done, he, like his predecessors, at first tried to avoid fighting France. In March 1891, after the initial clashes, Behanzin received French emissaries with apparently sincere expressions of friendship and desire for peace, and agreed not to make war on Porto Novo, since the French were there. But he refused formally to renounce his title to Cotonou, or his liberty to send armies to other parts of his dominions; and he rejected as infringing his internal sovereignty French demands for the release of some of his own subjects whom he had detained during the fighting. In 1892, after receiving new arms supplies from German merchants, he proudly reaffirmed his right to coerce all the towns which he considered as his, excepting Porto Novo, even at risk of a war with France.

> I am the king of the Negroes [he wrote to the French representative], and white men have no concern with what I do. . . . Please remain calm, carry on your trade at Porto Novo, and on that basis we shall remain at peace as before. If you want war I am ready. . . .

By this time the French had come to the conclusion, somewhat apprehensively and reluctantly, that war would be necessary to defend the position which their subjects had established in Dahomey. Accordingly, in 1892 the Senegalese Colonel A. A. Dodds carried out that march on Abomey which tough Dahomean diplomacy had thus far helped to postpone. But even now France hesitated to destroy the structure of the Dahomean state. During 1893 Behanzin continued to resist with much popular support; and the French, finding difficulty in identifying other *interlocuteurs valables,* contemplated accepting his offers to negotiate. In January 1894 they recognized his brother as ruler of an area corresponding roughly to the seventeenth-century rump of Abomey, and as a temporary expedient practised a form of indirect rule until 1900. Even afterwards the dynasty continued to enjoy widespread prestige, which the French acknowledged in 1928 by arranging the ceremonial return from exile of Behanzin's ashes. (One wonders how far they considered the implications of the analogy with the return of Napoleon's ashes to France in 1840.) Nor was this prestige confined to traditionalist circles. A clandestine newspaper published by two nationalist school-teachers in 1915 took the name *Le Recadaire* (ceremonial messenger) *de Behanzin.*

By comparison, Tofa's policy of collaboration won certain advantages in the short run. He remained ruler of Porto Novo under the French protectorate until his death in 1908, but with dwindling privileges and functions. He seems to have become bitterly conscious of accusations that he had sold his country to the French. With his funeral, say the traditional historians, the monarchy of Porto Novo came to an end. His heirs, for whom he had sought French support, were mere French clients, their influence among the Gun eclipsed by others. On 28 November 1965 the author of this essay visited Tofa's successor in Porto Novo. Elsewhere in the town revolutionary manifestations were taking place on behalf of the Gun president of the Dahomean Republic, who had been declared deposed by a Fon prime minister. Even though this constitutional conflict dearly reflected old antagonisms of Fon and Gun, however, the royal palace had become an irrelevant backwater. President S. M. Apithy, representative of the Gun "national cause," had begun his eventful political career as a young intellectual associated with the Catholic mission. But Justin Ahomadegbe, leader of the Fon, spoke not merely as a trade unionist, but as a member of the house of Behanzin.

Until more research has been done on the policies and aims of individual African states, a survey of this kind must be superficial and tentative. It is hardly profound to conclude that the most important element making for the survival of African polities under colonial rule was simply a strong sense of ethnic or political identity—the attachment of their subjects to what has been called the "national cause." This sense of identity tended to be strengthened when the rulers who represented it could point to some record of resistance to imperialism. This does not mean blind or reactionary opposition. Those leaders who achieved most for the national cause, whether immediately or in the longer run, combined military action with more or less discriminating attempts to find some basis for co-existence or collaboration. Indeed, their success in keeping old national causes alive has sometimes presented problems to modern leaders who seek to represent a broader form of nationalism.

A. B. Davidson

AFRICAN RESISTANCE TO THE SCRAMBLE AND TO EUROPEAN COLONIAL RULE

A. B. Davidson of Moscow University offers a brief survey of European-African conflict from the partition until the end of colonial rule in this short paper, read in Dar Es Salaam in 1965. While the published article is neither the most recent nor the most analytical on the subject, its very sweep suggests the broad dimensions by which the scramble and its effects can be incorporated into African history. The thesis of national resistance movements which Davidson offers provides historical continuity and contemporary relevance to the scramble and the emergence of modern Africa.

An attentive study of the history of popular resistance in Africa will inevitably prove that this struggle acted as one of the most important stimuli to historical development for the African peoples. This struggle has never ended because whenever oppression exists, resistance to this oppression exists as well; this resistance can change its character and forms but it never ceases.

In fact the character and effectiveness of the resistance which one or another people offered to a considerable extent defines the place this people has occupied in colonial empires: that is whether it became a protectorate or a colony or whether it was able to preserve its independence like Ethiopia. In other words, in the course of the struggle against the imposition of colonial rule each people

From A. B. Davidson, "African Resistance and Rebellion against the Imposition of Colonial Rule," in T. O. Ranger, ed. *Emerging Themes of African History* (Nairobi, 1968), pp. 177–184, 188. Used by permission of East African Publishing House.

founded positions from which in our days it waged a struggle for complete liberation.

This resistance left its mark on the most important internal processes of the development of African peoples. As a rule in the course of the resistance tendencies to change developed more quickly; for instance in some countries feudalism started gaining in strength much more rapidly than before.

In the course of resistance to colonialism, tribes which up to that time had lived more or less in isolation gradually began to comprehend the identity of their interests. Nationalities and large ethnic units formed more rapidly; the features of national self-consciousness were crystallizing. Tribal unions were being created; the rudiments of state organizations came into being. The active forces that led the struggle made use of the religions which existed at that time, for example Islam in Northern Africa. All these and many other processes were inseparably linked with the struggle against the imposition of colonial rule and therefore it is impossible to understand them without careful study of the resistance of every people. . . .

What are the stages of this struggle?

This question is inseparably linked with the more general division into periods of the history of Africa as a whole since the beginning of colonial penetration. For the whole continent (but of course not for each country taken separately) it should be possible to accept the following division into periods. The first stage is up to the 1870s when colonial rule was exercised only over 10 per cent of African territory. Then the period from the 1870s till about 1900 when this rule affected over 90 per cent of the territory. Next, the period from the beginning of the twentieth century up to the First World War, when the system of colonial rule and imperialist exploitation already had been brought to most parts of Africa. Then the epoch between the two world wars when the crisis of the colonial system and imperialism started. And lastly the period after the World War II, when this system was broken down and dozens of young states appeared in place of colonies.

At these different stages of African history the African struggle took different forms. Up to 1870 it often took the form of uprisings of slaves against slavers. It was the struggle of coastal, very often separate, tribes and peoples. Fortresses and strongholds were being built on the coasts, local peoples were being put into a dependent and subordinate position and did not want to accept it. The resistance of the Hottentots against the establishment of Dutch rule in the Cape of Good Hope started in the fifties of the seventeenth century. In other areas whole peoples refused to work for their conquerors. That was why colonial powers had to import to Africa, Indians, Malayans and representatives of other non-African peoples. Considerable armed conflicts began to arise by the end of this period, but only in those regions where colonization had penetrated very deeply (as in Northern Africa, in Ashanti and the south of the continent).

The period between 1870–1900 is usually thought of in Africa as a struggle between European powers competing against each other. But in reality at that time the struggle between imperialist countries was *much less bloody* than skirmishes between colonialists on one side and Africans on the other side. It was the time when tribal and feudal African societies showed the most decisive resistance to colonization; when Ethiopians defeated the Italian army near Adowa; when the Sudanese crushed the British army near Khartoum; when Zulus gained the victory over English forces. At the same time it was in that period that new forces were arising, and together with them new forms of struggle. This applies to those areas where colonialism had dominated at that time for more than one decade and traditional foundations—tribal and feudal—had been strongly shaken.

This process went furthest in Southern Africa. Hundreds of thousands of Africans were working there on European farms, in towns and miners' settlements. During this period it was possible to see in Southern Africa forms of struggle that appeared in other parts of Africa considerably later. There was for instance the protest against colonization that arose amidst African Christians leading to sectarian movements—the so-called "native churches." Associations of electors (African voters) in Cape Colony favored the emergence of the rudiments of national and political consciousness. The same part was played by the African press that was already being published in Cape Colony at that time. In the 1880s also the first, very timid attempts were made to set up organized working-class movements. At that time the first attempts to organize a strike of African workers were made; the first very weak political organization came into being.

From the end of the nineteenth century until the First World War the last great struggle against colonization within the tribal system took place in Africa—the rebellion of the Herero and the Hottentots, the "Maji-Maji" rising and others. But sometimes these rebellions differed from previous ones—this means that the traditions of a tribal society were falling to the ground. Thus in the course of the Zulu' rebellion in 1906 a great part was played by a native (Ethiopian) church, and the leader of the whole rebellion was a chief of one of the comparatively small tribes.

At that time also in many African countries there arose, still in embryonic forms, new forces—workers, an intelligentsia. In connection with them the first political organizations appeared. The African National Congress (South Africa) created in 1912 appears to have been the first political organization on the scale of a whole country. But the leadership of the liberation movement was still in the hands of tribal chiefs and elders.

In the period between the two wars colonial exploitation became stronger but at the same time a gradual accumulation of the forces of the liberation movement was going on. This was favored by the influence of revolutionary events in Russia and some other European countries. In many countries the leadership of the liberation movement passed into the hands of the intelligentsia and bourgeois elements. This can be easily observed in the activities of the political organizations which were often created after the pattern of the African National Congress (South Africa) and even took the same nature. Often, for instance, in Nyasaland or Rhodesia, political organizations were created on the base of welfare associations or other urban associations. At that time the last significant movements of religious sects took place for example in the Congo and some other countries. In many parts of the continent riots of peasants took place.

The workers' movement became stronger. The mining areas of the Transvaal during the first war years were disturbed by big strikes. In 1935 and 1940 tens of thousands of "Copper belt" miners went on strike. *The actions of the workers were not only class but anticolonial in character.* In South and North Africa Communist parties appeared and came out with a comprehensive program for the struggle against colonization. The Pan-African movement which manifested itself at four Pan-African congresses between the two wars witnesses the arising of connections between forces of resistance of different African countries.

The last period—the post-World War II years, saw not merely a resistance to the imposition of colonial rule, but a preparation and implementation of national liberation revolution aimed at the complete destruction of colonial regimes.

It goes without saying of course that this outlined scheme of division into periods is not final or complete. The history of an immense continent in its diversity cannot be put into the limits of any strict scheme. Resistance took different forms in different parts of Africa and at different stages of its history. Differences in the nature and methods of colonial policy of the *parent states* had an influence on the forms of resistance. Of course it is impossible to cover in one report all these stages of the history of liberation movements. That is why I consider it possible to limit my historiographical report and pay most attention to the period of "The Scramble for Africa." Apparently the organizers of the conference meant this too since they suggested the question "resistance to the imposition of colonial rule" as the topic of my report.

We can say that for the time being the studying of the question of the struggle of African people is still in embryo. As a matter of fact, historians have not really raised yet the problems of African resistance to colonialism. It is to be supposed that many rebellions are not yet known; that historians have not "discovered" them yet. Often we do not have concrete information about those rebellions that are considered an established fact. It is not discovered yet what were the motive forces of rebellions, how they were organized, why rebels undertook one or another action, what was the intercommunication between different events, linked with a rebellion. About other forms of resistance we know even less than about armed rebellions.

How does historiographical literature consider the question of the African peoples' resistance during the period of "The Scramble for Africa"? If we try to summarize the traditional, European historiographical view about the problem, first of all we shall find a frank defense of colonialism. According to one of these versions the African people apprehended the coming colonialist as good fortune; as deliverance from fratricidal internecine wars, from the tyranny of neighboring tribes, from epidemics, and periodic starvations. This school wrote about the peoples who did not resist as "peace loving." Other peoples who from the very beginning treated colonialism with such an evident enmity that it was impossible to hide this fact in literature were called "bloodthirsty" and readers were told that they merely imbibed with their mothers' milk a hatred of all "strangers." As is known European powers often explained their invasion as necessary to save "peace loving" people from their "bloodthirsty" neighbors. Later on both peoples—the one that was "saved" and the one that was "bloodthirsty" might rise together or at the same time against European newcomers. Thus in the 1890s Rhodes saved the Shona from the Ndebele, but in 1896 there broke out the almost simultaneous rebellion of both these peoples.

But facts of this kind did not modify the traditional scheme of interpretation which remained unchanged. According to another version which is not less widespread African chiefs without a moment's hesitation signed one-sided agreements and sold their lands and all the riches of their tribes for rum and beads. No doubt this sometimes happened. But there were many other cases. We know a great number of examples when chiefs and rulers of independent states entered upon diplomatic single combat with arch-colonial politicians who were not squeamish about the means they used. Skillfully and wisely they carried on negotiations and upheld the independence of their peoples at any rate for a certain period of time. Examples of this are Menelik II, Moshesh, Mutesa, Lobengula. The supporters of the beads and rum version, perhaps, idealize the colonialists in subtler ways—they openly admit the policy of lies and deceit, but they depict Africans as such primitive and irrational *semihuman beings* that the reader is prompted to accept the justice of the imposition of colonial rule.

In openly procolonial literature the struggle of Africans has been ignored. "The Scramble for Africa" was considered to be a struggle between imperialist powers only, and in these events Africans were given the part of an object, but not a subject. It was only the largest rebellions of Africans that were mentioned; the tendency existed to write only about so-called, "colonial wars" but authors did not understand or did not want to understand the nature of these wars. German, Portuguese, Italian and other historians did not call the wars their countries waged in African countries "predatory wars." On the other hand they ignored the fact that for Africans these wars were wars of independence.

While analyzing "colonial wars" they described as a rule the actions of European forces only. They described in detail what one or another column was doing, how and in what direction it moved. But the African remained a mass without a distinctive personality. Africans were mentioned only as an object of European troop actions. Authors as a rule wrote very little about the internal organization of African rebellions. Their readers cannot picture the rebels; what kind of people they were or what they were fighting for—what they felt—all these questions were unanswered. Europeans killed during these wars and rebellions were proclaimed national heroes. After Cecil Rhodes' war against the Matabele (1893), 36 Englishmen killed while trying to capture Lobengula were proclaimed national heroes and were built monuments. A heroic tragedy about their fate has been performed in British theaters. But the Matabele, who were really heroically defending the independence of their people, who were fighting with spears against maxim guns were only counted to the nearest thousand corpses. Again articles have appeared devoted to the question of whether General Gordon's fatal wound was a breast or a back wound. But the date and circumstances of Lobengula's death seem to be unknown up to now.

Authors who tried to explain African rebellions looked for their reasons to accidental or superficial circumstances. According to them rebellions were caused not by the interests of the whole tribe or people but by the yearnings of some part of this tribe. Often they took as this part the youngsters; the young warriors who desired "to wet their spears in blood" and to capture cattle for a marriage settlement. Very often misunderstandings were announced as the reason for a rebellion. Protectors of colonial rule refused to consider rebellion a regular phenomenon. They rejected the only correct explanation which regards rebellions as just wars for liberation, which is why they were supported by the overwhelming majority of Africans.

Colonial novels played a most painful part in the spreading of colonial theories. The formation of the traditional colonial literature was closely linked with racial theories. Colonial literature was born out of scornful treatment of the African peoples and in its turn favored the taking root of racial prejudices. Literature of this kind caused damage to the study of the African peoples' struggle because it spread wrong ideas. Documents and materials were not collected. Official European historiography didn't regard peoples' uprisings a subject that was worthy of serious studies.

It is necessary to note to the credit of Europeans that in the period when Africa was almost totally under colonial rule, there were some people in Europe and America that defended uprising colonial people. Among them there were famous writers, for instance, M. Twain, political figures, like N. Chernishevsky, publicists, like Morel, scientists, like Hobson. But their voices were not heard in official procolonial circles.

In that period the founders of Marxism took a clear position in their treatment of the African peoples' struggle. Engels wrote with admiration about the military skills and the art of war of Zulus in connection with the Anglo-Zulu War of 1879. Lenin wrote that the history of the 20th century, the century of unbridled colonialism, is full of colonial wars. But these colonial wars "were very often national wars of national rebellions of oppressed peoples." . . .

For the fruitful study of the history of African resistance and rebellion the efforts of progressive historians from all over the world are necessary. The history of Africa developed and is developing now in accordance with general laws of the history of other countries and continents. The African struggle against colonialism is inseparably linked with the struggle of the European peoples against capitalism and it is possible to understand the history of African resistance only in interdependence with the history of all mankind.

Suggestions for Additional Reading

With the recent and keen academic interest in African history the period of the partition has become the subject of a considerable number of monographs and broader reinterpretations, most of which are readily available in any large library. However, the student first encountering the subject might do well to begin in a traditional interpretive manner by turning to some of the standard treatments of modern European diplomacy. Of the many such volumes, three are easily, but advisedly, singled out: William Langer, *European Alliances and Alignments, 1871–1890* (New York, 1931); and another work by the same author, *The Diplomacy of Imperialism* (New York, 1931 and 2nd edition, 1960); then the study by A. J. P. Taylor, *The Struggle for Mastery in Europe, 1848–1918* (Oxford, 1954). These volumes provide a detailed analysis of the political problems affecting the European state system and also contain careful assessments of the overseas implications of growing European rivalries.

Of a similar sort but more closely addressed to the problems of imperialism are: Parker T. Moon, *Imperialism and World Politics* (New York, 1926; 17th printing, 1961), and Mary E. Townsend, *European Colonial Expansion since 1871* (Philadelphia, 1941). Both works are more concerned with a description of the various political aspects of the partition of Africa than with a general overview, although Moon's study does provide as an introduction a fulsome explanation of the causes of modern imperialism.

A number of recent studies have added new knowledge to and detailed assessments of the problems of imperialism in Africa. Two which combine the efforts of an international coterie of scholars have been coedited by Prosser Gifford and Wm. Roger Louis, *Britain and Germany in Africa* (New Haven, 1967), and *France and Britain in Africa* (New Haven, 1971). Both works contain superlative bibliographies which cover in detail the many aspects of European domination in Africa. Another volume of similar organization is *The History and Politics of Colonialism, 1870–1914,* which is Volume I of *Colonialism in Africa, 1870–1960,* ed. L. H. Gann and Peter Duignan (Cambridge, 1969). Gann and Duignan have also authored a more general work, *Burden of Empire: An Appraisal of Western Colonialism in Africa South of the Sahara* (London, 1968), which offers an interpretation that has been criticized for its rather Eurocentric bias. An exceptionally useful, brief introduction to the many dimensions of the partition, and one for which there is no equivalent in English, is Henri Brunschwig, *Le Partage de l'Afrique noire* (Paris, 1971).

Historical considerations of the general problem of expansion into Africa from a national perspective are numerous. For the role of Great Britain, Charles E. Carrington's *The British Overseas: Exploits of a Nation of Shopkeepers* (Cambridge, 1950), and Volume III of the *Cambridge History of the British Empire,* ed. E. A. Benians, James Butler and C. E. Carrington (London, 1959) are very helpful. W. David McIntyre, *The Imperial Frontier in the Tropics, 1865–1875* (London, 1967), offers an explanation of early British involvement in the affairs of West Africa which is supportive of the concept of "informal empire" and thus adds to the literature about the prelude to the scramble.

Unfortunately, no first-rate contemporary history of French imperialism exists at the moment in English. The older works include: Stephen Roberts, *A History of French Colonial Policy, 1870–1925* (London, 1927), which is most critical of the French colonial effort; and Herbert Priestley, *France Overseas: A Study in Modern Imperialism* (New York, 1938), which is a straightforward political assessment. Henri Brunschwig offers an interesting rebuttal of the economic interpretation of imperialism in his *French Colonialism, 1871–1914: Myths and Realities* (New York, 1966). Most recently, the subject of French motives in the scramble have been treated to close scrutiny in two significant monographs: A. S. Kanya-Forstner, *The Conquest of the Western Sudan: A Study in French Military Imperialism* (Cambridge, 1969); and Roger G. Brown, *Fashoda Reconsidered: The Impact of Domestic Politics on French Policy in Africa, 1893–98* (Baltimore 1969).

A variety of appraisals of German colonial policy is readily available. Of importance are Mary E. Townsend's two books: *The Origins of Modern German Colonialism* (New York, 1921), and *The Rise and Fall of the German Colonial Empire, 1884–1918.* Unlike A. J. P. Taylor, Miss Townsend sees Bismarck's colonial policy as genuinely assumed, and she fits German colonialism into the context of a growing German nationalism. William Aydelotte's *Bismarck and British Colonial Policy* (Philadelphia, 1937), is a very valuable monograph about West African policies and can be profitably read in connection with Townsend's and Taylor's works.

Moving from the European to the African setting, one finds that the quantity of material available on African history for this period has become almost abundant in recent years. A few general surveys are worthy of consideration here. Robert Cornevin's *Histoire de l'Afrique des Origines à Nos Jours* (Paris, 1956) attempts to embrace the whole of African history. While the quality of the work is generally high, there is very little innovation in the analysis of the "scramble." Two general texts recently available situate the partition in African history in a most effective way: Robert I. Rotberg, *A Political History of Tropical Africa* (New York, 1965); and Robert W. July, *A History of the African People* (New York, 1970).

Regional studies tend to offer much more to the student of the partition. First in order of significance is the recent magisterial study written by J. D. Hargreaves, *Prelude to the Partition of West Africa* (New York, 1963). Anyone desiring a detailed and thoughtful analysis of this complicated phase of the partition will find it here, and will find it presented in a very lucid fashion. Broader coverage in a much more general volume is found in Michael Crowder, *West Africa under Colonial Rule* (Evanston, 1968). Additional valuable reading on European activity in this region will be found in C. W. Newbury, *The West African Slave Coast and Its Rulers* (Oxford, 1961). J. D. Fage's *An Introduction to the History of West Africa* (Cambridge, 1962) is a very compact but thoughtful history which treats the partition in this region of Africa in terms of longer regional penetration by the European powers. Students interested in the broader history preceding the scramble in West Africa should also consult A. Adu Boahen, *Britain, the Sahara, and the West Sudan, 1788–1861* (Oxford, 1964). Two very important works which provide lucid interpretations of the entangled history of European rivalry in the upper Nile are: G. N. Sanderson, *A Study in the Partition of Africa: England, Europe and the Upper Nile, 1882–1889* (Edinburgh, 1965); and Robert O. Collins, *King Leopold, England and the Upper Nile, 1899–1909* (New Haven, 1968). A fine history of the east coast is that edited by Roland Oliver and Gervase Mathew, *A History of East Africa,* Volume I (London, 1968). In Chapter X, "The Wider Background to the Partition and Colonial Occupation," John Flint offers an intelligent interpretation of German motives and activities in this region and British response to them. Roland Oliver, *The Missionary Factor in East Africa* (London, 1952 and 1967) considers an important element in European penetration and domination in this region.

Most of the history written about Africa south of the Sahara centers around Boer and British policy in South Africa. The now classic study written by Cornelius de Kiewet, *The Imperialist Factor in South Africa, a Study in Politics and Economics* (Cambridge, 1937) is still a worthwhile introduction. Eric A. Walker, in his *A History of Southern Africa* (London, third edition, 1962), discusses the partition in Chapter XII, entitled, "The Scramble, 1881–96." A recent study which provides a fine background to British policy during the partition is John S. Galbraith, *Reluctant Empire: British Policy on the South African Frontier, 1834–1854* (Berkeley, 1963). As the title suggests, Galbraith argues that British policy was a reluctant response to Boer expansion. The growing antagonism between Boer and Briton, which finally led to the Boer War, is treated in the Problems in European Civilization series by Theodore Caldwell, *The Anglo-Boer War* (1965), which contains a useful bibliography. Further reading of Robinson and Gallagher, *Africa and the Victorians,* would here be profitable.

The Congo policy of Leopold II has received considerable attention. A good, but not particularly inspiring introductory history is Ruth Slade, *King Leopold's Congo* (Oxford, 1962). The Belgian historian Père A. Roeykens has written several books on this subject. In his *Leopold II et l'Afrique, 1880–1885* (Brussels, 1958) he attempts to explain the motives behind Leopold's actions. In opposition to the Stengers interpretation, recapitulated in the review appearing in this volume, Roeykens appraises Leopold's work as that of a Belgian patriot seeking the greater glory of his country. British policy in the Congo is carefully traced by Roger Anstey in *Britain and the Congo in the Nineteenth Century* (Oxford, 1962).

Any scholarly appreciation of the partition should include, of course, the biographies and writings of the explorers and adventurers who were greatly responsible for the carving up of the continent. Among the most obvious are the several accounts written by Stanley, notably: *Through the Dark Continent* (New York, 1879, 2 volumes), and *The Congo and the Founding of the Free State* (New York, 1885, 2 volumes). On other figures, there are: Margery Perham, *Lugard: the Years of Authority, 1898–1945* (London, 1960); James Flint, *Sir George Goldie and the Making of Nigeria* (Oxford, 1960); Roland Oliver, *Sir Harry Johnston and the Scramble for Africa* (London, 1957); and Felix Gross, *Rhodes of Africa* (London, 1956).

Periodicals worth perusing are: *Africa, African Affairs,* the *Journal of African History,* and *African Historical Studies.*